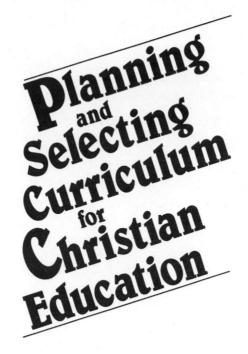

Planning and Selecting Curriculum for Christian Education

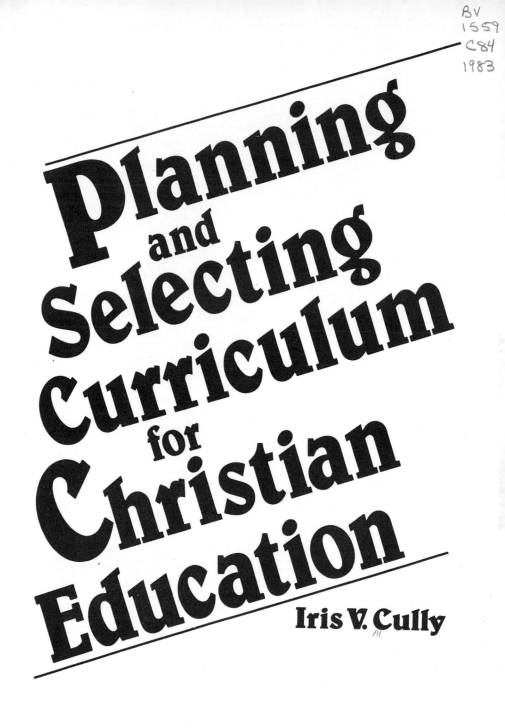

Planning and Selecting Curriculum for Christian Education

Iris V. Cully

Judson Press ® Valley Forge

PLANNING AND SELECTING CURRICULUM FOR CHRISTIAN
EDUCATION

Copyright © 1983
Judson Press, Valley Forge, PA 19481

The Scripture quotations in this publication are from the Revised Standard
Version of the Bible copyrighted 1946, 1952 © 1971, 1973 by the Division
of Christian Education of the National Council of the Churches of Christ
in the U.S.A., and used by permission.

Library of Congress Cataloging in Publication Data

Cully, Iris V.
  Planning and selecting curriculum for Christian education.

  1. Christian education—Curricula. 2. Curriculum planning. I. Title.
BV1559.C84   1983   268'.6   82-18752
ISBN 0-8170-0987-6

For Kendig Brubaker Cully
In celebration of the many years of
joyful collaboration

Contents

Preface

Curriculum is on the mind of everyone involved in religious education. Teachers in local churches are certain that the *right* curriculum would solve all of their problems. People who publish and edit materials hope that carefully written courses will go far toward improving the quality of religious education.

Both put too much hope in one strand of the educational enterprise. Their concern, however, highlights the importance of the work. Surprisingly little formal writing has been offered in the area in recent years. D. Campbell Wyckoff's *The Curriculum of Christian Education* (1954) outlined a model for curricular development that has been basic for published curriculum materials during the past twenty years. The National Council of Churches' curriculum development project in the 1960s was followed by the ambitious programs of the Joint Educational Development team. Roman Catholic materials have been written from a less consciously theoretical base and in recent years have been based on the assumption that most parish teaching will rely on volunteer teachers.

This book will explore the issues to be faced in the process of curriculum construction, whether on the national or local level. Accepting the validity of current thinking that every facet of church life is part of a total system, these chapters will examine the specific subsystem within religious education known as the curriculum.

Readers are first invited to explore the various options available for building a curriculum. A second chapter will help both producers and users of curriculum materials to view their differences, probe the reasons for these differences, and explore ways of achieving mutual understanding. This rapprochement will be fostered more concretely in a chapter that describes the work of individuals in the process.

Subsequent chapters help readers gather the kind of information needed for making careful curricular choices: how to state goals and how to structure evaluation; how to examine theological and educational assumptions; and how to bring together the many types of learning that comprise education.

The writer is confident that those who read these pages and pause to apply each chapter to their local situations will have a basis for making informed decisions about curriculum building. People on the judicatory and national levels may be helped to see more clearly the problems and criticisms that curriculum users have when materials are transposed from the written page to the parish situation. Those who teach courses in religious education, for laity or for professionals, will for the first time in many years have a book to provide them with a basic text on curriculum.

It is hoped that this book will provide a forum where all who are involved in the church's teaching ministry may be able to understand one another better and to realize their interdependence in developing the curriculum for teaching.

Iris V. Cully
Lexington Theological Seminary
Lexington, Kentucky

Chapter

The Curriculum Quest

The choice of curriculum materials is a perennial concern for everyone who works in an educational setting. State commissions set curricular standards for the public schools. School committees investigate textbooks. Local schools choose books, and teachers use them. Then students of all ages are taught from these materials.

So it is in churches. In some Protestant Sunday church schools or Roman Catholic CCD (Confraternity of Christian Doctrine) programs, curriculum materials may be the largest item in the budget. Ordering curriculum becomes a major task. Awaiting its arrival causes anxious moments (Will it arrive before the first session?). Teachers are enthusiastic—or they complain. Parents want to know the subject matter. Closets in churches are filled with outdated and unused curricular material. Some teachers receive their materials and never open the teacher's book, preferring their own outlines. Other teachers read the manual but interpret what they read in an individualized way. How can one make any sense out of a project that requires so much time and money but that seldom seems to be generally satisfying?

A beginning can be made by asking what is meant by the word "curriculum." In the broadest definition, curriculum includes both the materials and the experiences for learning. The textbook or manual is the starting point, but enrichment books, filmstrips, recordings, and workbooks are other elements. Some people would include all the experiences of a learner as part of the curriculum. Attending Sunday worship is such an experience and could well be integrated into the curriculum.

More specifically, curriculum refers to the written courses of study generally used for religious education. The focus of concern in most parishes is the curriculum used for Sunday church school or CCD classes. Courses of study are also available for youth and adult groups, weekday religious education, vacation church school, camps, conferences, and retreats. Such materials need not be confined to use only in the settings originally intended but may become resource materials for other settings.

Materials vary in the time span required for their use. Some include fifty-two sessions—enough material to be used weekly through an entire year. Other materials may be planned for a weekend or for each day for a week. Vacation church school materials usually require daily sessions for one or two weeks. Study materials may be written for a group that will meet monthly throughout the year or weekly for a limited number of weeks.

In addition to the time required to complete the course, another consideration is the block of time allotted for each session. This may range from a Sunday church school class of thirty minutes to one that can be expanded to sixty minutes or longer, perhaps correlating with the worship service.

Age span is another factor to be considered in choosing or developing curricular materials. Some courses are closely graded, which means that they are designed for pupils of the same age or in the same grade in school. Other courses are group graded for use with a two-year or a three-year age span. A broadly graded curriculum is designed to be adaptable to a wide age span: preschool, elementary school age (grades one to six), junior high (grades seven to nine), high school (grades nine to twelve), college age, or young adult group.

Most adult materials are designed with the assumption that adults of any age will find the materials usable. In practice, this does not usually follow. Some churches have a tradition of separate groups for young adults, young couples, middle-aged adults, and older adults. Frequently such groups have maintained their identity for many years and are friendship and mutual support groups as much as they are educational groups. When several different courses are offered, subject matter and methods are chosen in order to attract specific age groups to each course of study.

There are also intergenerational materials, designed to bring together people of all ages—from children through older adults. Such lessons are based on themes broad enough and contain methods flexible enough so that all can enjoy one another's company and share insights. Such materials have been developed only recently, but the intergenerational parish gathering has a long history rooted in events such as the church supper and the Christmas bazaar.

Setting, time span, and age of participants are three elements in the design of curricular materials. How does one make a choice among available options? This is a pertinent question today when the tradition of staying loyally with a prescribed curriculum seems to be on the wane.

Precursors

About a century ago Sunday church school materials had proliferated to such an extent that this was called the "Babel" period. Into that chaos stepped two able persons: a Methodist pastor, John H. Vincent (later a bishop), and a Chicago Baptist layman, B. F. Jacobs. Accepting the premise that biblical study was the basis for the Sunday church school, they worked with others to devise an outline through which, it was affirmed, one could cover basic biblical material in seven years. The lessons were carefully chosen, and the outline became known as the International Uniform Lesson Series. It is still very much alive, but today it comprises a five-year cycle and is set up by an interdenominational committee under the auspices of the National Council of Churches.

Annual study guides for the use of the Uniform Lesson Series were first published a century ago. The tables of contents of these books give some idea of the overarching plan of the series.[1] There are not only carefully written lesson plans for youth and adults but also suggestions for sermons and teacher training.

Today few curricula use the Uniform outlines as the basis for lesson plans at every age level. Some use the outlines only for adolescents and adults although the outlines have been modified for use with children.

The advantage of the Uniform Lesson Series had been that it gave consistency to the courses of study within a local church. If the teacher of a children's class were suddenly to be absent, a member of an adult class would be familiar enough with the material to substitute as teacher, needing only to adapt the teaching methods to young learners. A minister could offer teacher training to all teachers weekly or monthly (as some still do), helping them to probe the meaning of the passage to be taught on the following Sunday. Study resources would be usable by all teachers and by adult students, and a library of study resources could be acquired gradually.

Early in the twentieth century, teachers of children realized that the Uniform Lesson Series outlines were not meeting the needs of their pupils. They were becoming aware of child development theories and showed a growing interest in age-level educational methods. Religious education leaders began to inquire about how children grow spiritually. This led them to look for biblical materials that might be specifically helpful for boys and girls in each stage of development.

Group-graded lessons were the outcome of this inquiry. Children ages four to five were designated "beginners." (Nursery classes did not have a special curriculum until several decades later.) Primary classes were for children ages six to eight, and junior children were ages nine to eleven. Intermediates were ages twelve to fourteen and seniors, ages fifteen to seventeen. School grade designations were seldom used.

This three-year system has continued, with modifications, to the present. However, some curricula have been based on a two-year grading span because editors believed that the differences, for example, between a first grade child and a third grade child make it difficult for one group to meet the needs of each age. Other curricula have been based on a broad age span with groups formed according to abilities rather than ages. This makes possible more individual attention to students, as teachers work with one level of ability in a class rather than with many ability levels. The ages included in a high school group have frequently been decided by whether the high school of a particular community is a three- or four-year high school. Intermediate school or junior high is another flexible age span.

Religious educators eventually moved toward the use of a closely graded system that would have a course for children at each grade level, much as the schools have. Large Sunday schools had enough children so that the narrow separation could be functional. Instead of dividing a large group of children into separate classes, each of which would be studying the same material, they reasoned, why not give each age group distinctive material? Thus a closely graded series was developed and for many years was the joint project of several denominations. The tradition of several denominations working together in curriculum development is a long one that has had ups and downs, but today is being reestablished.

At about the same time that the Uniform Lesson Series was being developed, Roman Catholic catechetics took a new turn with the decree of the Third Plenary Council of bishops (1884) that resulted in a revised catechism, long known as the Baltimore Catechism. Inevitably there were criticisms from users, but the Baltimore Catechism formed the basis for religious instruction in Catholic schools until it too was revised in 1941.

Although all Catholic education was intended to occur in private or parochial schools, eventually a recognition of the number of Catholic children in public schools led to the formation of Confraternity of Christian Doctrine (CCD) classes, held after public school hours. Staffed by members of religious orders who taught in parochial schools and by lay people, these instructional periods were based on the catechism, and materials were developed with methods suited to age groupings. Dissatisfaction with the narrowness of the content eventuated, especially after Vatican II, in a creative surge in curricular materials that explore faith in biblical, theological, and experiential terms. Materials are usually closely graded, reflecting large parishes with large numbers of children in each age group. Courses of study include materials for once-a-week CCD sessions and longer, parochial school sessions. An emphasis on adult religious education is new and has resulted in some innovative approaches.

Curriculum Options

It was said earlier that an examination of the bookshelves in many churches would indicate that some curriculum materials are never used. Why does this happen? What is used as a replacement? These are important questions.

A teacher may have valid personal reasons for ignoring or rejecting the material chosen: it is too easy or too difficult for the pupils; it does not provide enough help for the teacher or activity for pupils; it is not biblical enough—or it is too biblical; it has a viewpoint with which the teacher disagrees. The replacement usually is a course of the teacher's own choosing, with no reference to the total teaching context of the parish. Churches try to deal with such situations through various options.

Publishers spend large sums for research to find out what is needed and wanted. They offer outlines that have been developed after several years of work by professionals in the field.

They assign writers to specific courses and then edit this material. Books are made attractive through the work of illustrators and designers. Promotion of the material is planned so that people can know what is available. Printing and distribution are major enterprises.

A parish may use one complete curriculum for all classes. This has much to commend it. One value of using a single curriculum is the consistency that it gives to the educational program. The material is graded, repetition is structured in a deliberate way so that a subject can be explored in different dimensions at each age level. Overall planning has already established the study areas to be included in all courses and the specific materials to be written for each area. Learning areas are based on needs and capabilities of students at various ages.

For example, it is not enough to say that a course of study will include the Old Testament. Decisions have to be made concerning key persons, ideas, and events that can be realistically included in a total curriculum. Then it must be determined which of these persons, ideas, and events can be understood by learners at six years, ten, sixteen, or adulthood.

These materials must also be related to the life needs and experiences of learners. Given the possibility that a basic understanding of the Bible and its relation to the Christian life may be received through Sunday church school or CCD attendance between the ages of three and eighteen years, what materials would be so essential for teaching in these settings that adults with such a background would have some primary understandings for biblical study?

A total curriculum of this kind will have a consistent approach to educational theory with attention paid to developmental stages of learning, appropriate methods, and various means of relating the material to life. Then pupils can begin each year comfortable with the educational approach to be used because it is consistent with what they have experienced.

Such a curriculum also has a consistent theological and biblical understanding. This is essential if learners are to develop skills for biblical interpretation. Publishers of curriculum materials, whether from denominational or private sources, are clear about these presuppositions and will usually outline such information in the first pages of the teacher's manual. It is confusing for a learner to be given different theological approaches, being taught one year "This is what the Bible says; accept it" and the next year "This is what the Bible says; how would you interpret it?" and again "This is what the Bible says; and this is how to interpret it." Faith and assurance are not built that way.

A total curriculum also has drawbacks. Unfortunately, there is not always the consistency in writing that one would expect. Many writers are involved, and editors may be limited in their ability to revise material. The curriculum is designed to be used everywhere in the country, in churches of many sizes, and with classes that vary widely in the number of pupils. The educational and cultural settings are as varied as are the geographical settings. It is almost impossible to supply material that could meet so many needs.

Finally, competency among the teachers using the material will vary. Some come with a background in teaching. Others have taken up a task for which they feel unprepared. Some desire the freedom to develop individualized sessions from suggested materials, while others want to know exactly what to do, step by step. Some welcome the use of extra resources, and others teach in situations where such resources would not be readily available. No course of study could ever meet such a wide variety of situations. Every course needs to be revised for the specific setting in which it is to be used.

This realization leads some churches to reject the idea of using one total course of study. They have decided that if so much adaptation is necessary, it would be better to take a broader approach. One solution is to build units of study around selected themes. A planning committee chooses the themes and decides what kind of materials and experiences would comprise an adequate religious education program for the learners in their parish, ages three to eighteen, for example. Then the committee maps the cycles in which these themes will be taught. There might be three to five themes repeated each year with different materials and experiences, or the themes could be repeated over a two- or three-year cycle.

The next step is to examine curriculum catalogues, select the materials that have such courses, and order them. If, for example, it is decided that worship will be a theme at the early childhood level when children are beginning to attend the worship service, at middle childhood level in order to deepen the children's understanding of worship, and at junior high level when youth may be preparing for church membership, the planning committee must find materials to meet these needs.

Once the selected materials arrive, other questions must be answered as the committee examines the materials. Are the suggested resources readily available? Does their content interpret correctly the denomination's understanding of worship? Are the available courses appropriate for the learning level of the children in the parish? Would the teachers be capable of using the methods included in the materials? After specific course materials are selected, the other materials ordered for examination may be retained for a teachers' resource shelf.

Although such a curriculum is not bought as a package (that is, as the product of one publisher), it has unity in addition to particularity; namely, it presents the themes that are viewed as important to that church, has theological and educational consistency, and fits the capabilities of the church's pupils and teachers.

Some parishes have adopted an extreme method of developing a curriculum by writing their own. This is difficult because it requires starting from "scratch." The decision to undertake this task rests on the premises that their situation is unique and the skill of the planners is extensive. It occurs when a parish has decided that no extant curriculum can fill its needs theologically or experientially. Some churches want a curriculum that meets their criterion of theological consistency that neither denominational nor independent publishers seem able to fulfill. Others feel constricted by the formality of existing curricula and want experience-oriented learning that they think can best be developed locally. Some wish to develop a curriculum around the Bible, but instead of using the Uniform Lesson Series outline, they want to use a three-year lectionary.

The value of a locally or regionally developed curriculum lies in the opportunity it offers for participation by planners, writers, and teachers. Inasmuch as we learn by doing, this is unquestionably a learning experience for those who do it.

The drawbacks arise from the oversimplification implied by a non-professional approach. If writing varies in quality in published curriculum where editors know a network of writers, it will surely vary in an experimental curriculum. While consistency of purpose (theological and educational) may be a goal, good communication skills are necessary so that this purpose can be translated into usable materials. If the ability of learners at each age level is a constant concern for professional curriculum developers, it will be a problem for parish curriculum writers.

If teaching methods are difficult to select and present in professionally written materials, they would be no easier for an informally produced course of study.

The most serious practical problem, however peripheral it may seem to those who are designing their ideal curriculum, is the amateurish, and often unattractive appearance of the material. The cost of production usually precludes the use of printing, and mimeographing has to be of a high quality in order to be clear. Developing an attractive format in predominantly word-oriented material requires aesthetic skill. The lack of color makes materials uninviting to both pupils and teachers, and illustrations are limited in quantity.

Some independently developed courses of study for adults can be set up attractively enough so that these aesthetic limitations are minimized. Adults are accustomed to instructional materials in many forms. They receive such at work and through the mail. However, surveys of Sunday church school teachers have indicated that format (meaning color, illustration, and page layout) is an important consideration in the choice of materials. Some courses have been rejected because of format, even before the content was explored.

Another approach to curriculum found in some churches is the "free choice" approach. Each teacher chooses a course of study that he or she feels comfortable using. As a result of this process, sometimes no one, including the minister, knows what courses are included in the total curriculum. The result is similar to the situation that occurs when curriculum material chosen for the whole church is ignored by one or more teachers. Such a school ends up with parts of two or more curricula in use.

The advantage of this "free choice" approach is that each teacher is satisfied with the self-chosen course of study. The disadvantages are a lack of correlation in class materials and a lack of consistency in theological and educational approaches. Such a procedure, however helpful in maintaining a full teaching staff, undermines the learning process because there is no consistent reinforcement of what is taught; pupils could be presented with the same material in two consecutive years and receive two different approaches to biblical interpretation. Sometimes this indicates that the educational task is not taken seriously by the whole church or that the church is indifferent to what is taught. Or it may mean that teachers do not view themselves as part of the whole teaching ministry.

Although general consistency is needed for a curriculum, a variety of educational and theological approaches, when deliberately chosen, can be useful for adult education. Adults differ widely in backgrounds and interests. They need to have such class options as lecture presentation, intellectual discussion, mutual sharing and support, and research and inquiry.

The subjects they wish to pursue may cover a wide spectrum, and only a few published curricula offer much choice in adult courses. Several denominations, however, do publish a wealth of elective units for adult study in different categories, including Bible, theology, social concerns, and personal religious living.[2] Further explorations and the "grapevine" ("In the place where I lived three years ago, we found the most interesting course. . . .") will uncover some little-known experimental courses. Unfortunately there is no directory through which these may be found. Some courses deserve oblivion; others should be more widely distributed.

Independently developed curriculum also finds favor among adolescents, although it is more widely used for informal (usually Sunday afternoon or evening) sessions. Adolescents are accustomed to being offered electives at school, and a Sunday church school class that offers no options may elicit their resentment, usually exhibited as indifference. One possibility is for the leader to work with the young people to select themes, develop units, collect resources (persons, films, books/articles, and so forth), and explore an area for a specific number of sessions. Another option is to find materials that have been published on the jointly selected themes and choose a course of study from them. One factor in the decision will be the availability of resources for developing the course. It may be more practical to choose one already prepared.

Issues Affecting Curriculum Choices

Three modes of curricular development have been explored: using a complete curriculum produced by one publisher; developing themes and collecting material from varied sources; or writing a curriculum for a parish. Each of these options raises questions that need further consideration.

Under what circumstances would the first option—a complete curriculum—be a viable option? Some denominational publishers have found that a startlingly small percentage (under 50 percent) of their congregations use the "official" curriculum in its entirety. This should not surprise anyone who realizes the diversity in size, geographical setting, and theological interpretations within any one main line denomination. There are a large number of evangelical members within any of the denominations belonging to the National Council of Churches. These hold in common a liberal spirit, since they remain within the confessional family, but the numbers suggest that a curriculum that is not conservative in its biblical interpretation will not be acceptable among these congregations. This is also true among Roman Catholic parishes, but they do not have an "official" curriculum.

A slight move in the direction toward affirming differences has been made in the development of the Christian Education: Shared Approaches (CE:SA) curriculum by a coalition of twelve denominations. Each of the four approaches is predicated on a different mode of biblical interpretation, although evangelicals will hardly see much movement in their direction theologically. Each approach is designed for all age levels, either on a two- or three-year cycle. Each develops different teaching styles. In this way, several criticisms of a unified curriculum are met.

The most successful continuing exponents of the unified curriculum are the independent publishers. They have perfected the art of knowing what many people want and of appealing to as many different needs as can be consistent with volume publishing. The curriculum is built on a two- or three-year, group-graded cycle, and session plans include specific suggestions to help teachers adapt materials to both the youngest and the oldest in the class. This is especially helpful to small membership churches that must include children of several ages in a class in order to have satisfying groups. While the total enrollments, nationally, of such churches may be smaller than that of large churches, the number of classes involved (and teachers) is larger. These publishers and their materials are well known to a large number of Protestant churches of many denominations.

Editors have concentrated on making the material simple to teach. Most lessons can be taught, if necessary, with only a cursory reading of the material before the session. They are carefully written so that the teacher can visualize the steps in order. All follow a formula outline for the development of a session that is consistent throughout the whole curriculum. All include in the materials whatever resources are needed for teaching. Because most volunteer teachers are untrained and may sometimes go to class unprepared, despite the fondest hopes of religious educators, such materials have wide appeal. Most churches, particularly those with small memberships, have little access to auxiliary resources; so the self-contained aspect of the material is important.

The courses have a simple and consistent approach to the Bible. To begin with, the biblical story is central to each lesson, and its application to life is clear. Teacher and learner are not expected to interpret the material theologically (For example, the question "What do you think the writer of this passage meant?" would not be asked.) but may simply apply the story to everyday life. The theological viewpoint as expressed in the story and commentary is consistently conservative. There may be several classic "theories" of atonement, but these Sunday church school materials know only one: the substitutionary theory that Jesus died for your sins. Writers avoid social justice issues and do not encourage wide-ranging discussion of the ramifications of personal decision making. Right and wrong are usually presented in a clear-cut fashion. This consistency is a strengthening prop for many teachers who themselves have not thought of the implications of theological or biblical statements.

Is it good to have so simple an approach to Christian education? Those persons whose cultural and educational backgrounds incline them to welcome paradox, controversy, and the tension of weighing alternatives will be uncomfortable. They will look for other options. Should denominational publishers' curriculum compete with the independent publishers by taking their route? The diversity within each denomination would preclude this. Can the denominational publishers continue to produce materials that appeal only to the "liberal" segment? Their unique contribution has been through a philosophy of curriculum building that encourages the creative teacher and the curious learner. Is such an approach financially feasible, and can (or should) a denomination finance it? These are serious questions.

How viable is the second option of choosing themes and assembling a curriculum from available resources? It requires people with appropriate skills who are able to develop a curriculum consistent with the needs of a particular parish. These skills include the abilities to choose courses with which individual teachers will feel comfortable, to know the church's theological/biblical stance clearly enough to find compatible materials, and to find a sufficient number of available courses to sustain the theme.[3] Developing units for teaching requires the sustained efforts of people who can set goals, evaluate materials, collect resources, and plan continuing teacher development.

The unit approach usually presupposes content as the basis for curriculum, although courses could be built around learner experiences and concerns, bringing the resources of the faith to meet the needs at each age level. However, few published materials can fulfill the latter quest. This fact may say more about present trends in curriculum publishing than about the legitimacy of the approach.

What place is there for the experimental curriculum, the "do-it-yourself" project? At its best, this evokes the creative talents of many people willing to assess the specific needs of learners in a particular setting. It requires educational and theological skills as well as willingness to spend time collecting resources and to engage in constant evaluation. This approach may be chosen by people who want to float freely, who react to customary options that seem too rigid. They want to develop curriculum as they go along and to explore viewpoints more broadly than they have found possible in printed materials. On an adult level, this approach may be inviting and enriching. In working with adolescents, it can be stimulating for skilled teachers and inquiring students. With children it will be most viable in a community where children are already accustomed to experimental approaches in their daily schooling.

An experimental curriculum may be seen as a solution to the problem of people who have a specific viewpoint to inculcate and can find no materials adequate to the purpose. It may be more rigidly designed than already printed materials, and it has sometimes been the brainchild of a pastor critical of the theological or biblical approaches available in other materials.

An experimental curriculum may bring a wealth of resources to the learning process, or it may make do with mimeographed outlines and few materials, none of the kinds of format usually so appealing to teachers. The curriculum may be enthusiastically received and even become the basis for a more widely circulated course of study, or it may last only as long as the people who designed it are willing to stay with the project.

The important consideration for curriculum planners is to know the pros and cons of the options, to explore the kinds of materials available for carrying out each one, and to determine what combination is best for their situations.

One thing is certain. No longer is it possible to say that there is only one way of choosing curriculum. There isn't even one easy way because any choice involves work both in the choosing and in the teaching.

Chapter

Issues in Curriculum Development

Reasons for the variety of curriculum options taken by parishes are many, but one is philosophy. Philosophy is present in the conflict between what is and what could be, the real and the ideal. Concerned people in congregations view curriculum in a practical way. Professional religious educators tend to begin with principles. People in churches need to be aware of how the professionals are thinking and need to voice concerns to them as both strive toward improved teaching materials.

In most denominations two departments are involved in religious education. One provides leadership in the specialized areas of ministry to children, youth, adults, families, and minorities and special services, such as resources and programs. The other is concerned with the publication of curricular materials. The two departments may be in the same building, or in two different cities. In some cases, one department handles both functions. Usually both departments are staffed with professionally trained people whose educational backgrounds have been in theology and religious education. They have agreed on a common viewpoint and work toward common goals.

The unfortunate fact is that people in the churches rarely have the same kind of educational background. They may not understand and so may be suspicious of some of the ways by which the denominational staff people want to fulfill the goals with which, in general, all would agree. When materials that represent advanced thinking in biblical studies and religious education appear in print, some churches react negatively. They choose one of the options outlined earlier, designing their own units or writing a new curriculum.

Developing Usable Curriculum

A long-standing goal of curriculum to which educators have addressed themselves is that of applying the Bible to life situations. However, most people prefer to do Bible study rather than to use the Bible as a resource from which to deal with life situations. If they are willing to use the Bible as a resource, then they would rather apply the Bible to personal living situations than to societal situations. When these expectations are disregarded by denominational leaders in education, churches become dissatisfied and withdraw from programs.

Teachers sensitive to the needs of children can be satisfied with a curriculum for preschool children that alternates biblical and life-experience materials with applicable biblical verses to anchor the life-situational material. However, few teachers are comfortable with materials that are basically life-oriented using biblical materials as resources.[1]

Sometimes church people feel that denominational staff persons are out of touch with the constituency and are unresponsive to their needs. It could be that the needs perceived by the professionals are not the same as the needs felt in the parishes.

Denomination staff people may have caught a vision of what they conceive to be an optimum curriculum. They want to improve materials so that the curriculum will give learners a deeper understanding of the Bible and a fuller awareness of what it means to live as a Christian. They know that there are many factors in a person's Christian development, of which written curriculum is only one, but they perceive this material to be strategic.

They also know that a church's choice of curriculum is a bellwether of parish attitudes toward religious education. Sometimes the number of parishes using denominational curricula has represented less than 50 percent of the constituency. If the volume of sales has any significance as a criterion for evaluation, there is a message here.

Denominational curriculum planners feel a responsibility for improving materials. Questionnaires have been devised and distributed to the people who use materials. They are asked to respond with their preferences on format, use of the Bible, teaching methods, and so on. Their replies are helpful indicators for improving the materials, although the final answer is given in the number of curriculum orders.

Careful planning goes into new curriculum and ways of introducing people to new curriculum. Professionals know that new materials are more easily accepted when help is given in their use and teacher-training sessions, designed for an area, community, or parish, are often offered for this reason. For those who cannot or will not attend such meetings, some help is found in the introductory pages of the teacher's manual. Teachers will find that it is always wise to study this material before reading specific session plans.

Independent publishers design materials to meet people's felt needs. They do not challenge any biblical or theological assumptions. They may avoid materials that deal with biblical origins and biblical interpretation. They do not have the concern that denominational educators have to encourage inquiry and new insights. If the materials do raise ethical questions, learners may be offered immediate answers in the Scripture. The ambiguity of moral choice is not pressed. Such material appeals to people who feel comfortable with their present belief systems, but it does not encourage growth.

These publishers do not usually try to induce teachers to use untried methods or to go looking for outside resources. Assuming correctly that many teachers are new, the editors give them simple methods, provide worksheets for pupil use, and confine the lesson plans to materials in a packet with suggestions for supplementary materials as an option. The methods are those with which children are familiar from school, and the techniques, those that mothers have used with children on rainy days at home.

These publishers have a staff of well-trained editors with either educational or theological background. The editors' most important skill is that of seeing a teacher's book through the eyes of an untrained teacher and editing so clearly that the material is easy to follow. Auxiliary materials may be purchased along with the courses of study: magazines, letters to parents, and songbooks. The field staff are salespersons who know the material and know how to use it but are not necessarily competent to give other religious education counsel. However helpful they may be to volunteer teachers, these publishers are frequently perceived as a threat by denominational publishing houses.[2]

All Roman Catholic materials are produced by independent publishers. These frequently attempt to meet the needs of both the professional teacher and the CCD teacher. Some are textbook publishers for whom this is one segment of their total market.

Developing Loyalty

Curriculum departments of denominations appeal to churches for loyalty. "We belong to a particular household of faith," they say. "You need to know about it and feel a part of it in order to understand the varieties of religious faith and experience in our culture." Each denomination is a "family" and has an "ethos." One of the ways that this is conveyed is through the materials for religious education. These explain what "we" stand for biblically, theologically, and educationally. This is a factor to be considered when choosing independently published materials.

Another plea for loyalty is made based on the need for financial support. No publishing venture can continue without support from a faithful constituency that subscribes to its materials year after year. This basic group has to be large enough and must spend enough money so that the venture breaks even or makes a profit. No private enterprise could continue without such support. The Standard Publishing Company, a popular supplier of Sunday church school materials, is part of the Standex conglomerate and would be unlikely to remain in existence unless it produced a profit. The David C. Cook Publishing Company is now a nonprofit organization whose foundation subsidizes specific religious education development programs.

The denominational curriculum enterprise, however, is also a service project to the constituency. The production of curriculum is part of its work in religious education. It needs to make a profit but can survive for a while without doing so if a balance has been accumulated.

Another argument that has been made for using a denominational curriculum is the theological one. The sixteenth century split in the Western church resulted in numerous branches within the Protestant sector: some national churches, others independent churches. In the United States, and to some extent in Canada, such groups proliferated. Anyone can find a religious group that stresses his or her particular theological tenets.

The "main line" denominations consider themselves to be liberal in the sense that they encourage theological inquiry. They may subscribe to the classic creedal statements and still assume broad interpretations. One way in which this openness is encouraged is through study materials, particularly at the youth and adult level.

Can the open stance of a denomination continue indefinitely

without educational materials that support it? This becomes a serious question when one realizes that Sunday church school teachers learn more from the materials they teach than do their students. It is the teachers' approach to faith that is formed by the material. Thus, a teacher's manual is a primary resource for adult education. Churches need to give thought to this factor.

Another question must be raised: Can any denominational material meet the theological needs of its whole constituency? The Southern Baptist Convention has some twelve million members to be served, and the United Methodist Church has ten million members. The Roman Catholic Church, with more than forty million members, has no official materials and a broad spectrum of materials from independent publishers.

Denominational curriculum materials attempt to reflect theological viewpoints that represent the majority of constituents. Members who prefer more conservative or more liberal materials seek these elsewhere. No denominational material can possibly appeal on a theological/biblical basis to the whole constituency.

Another basic question is what teaching methods should be used in curriculum materials. A liberal or inquiring spirit is best fostered through the use of methods of inquiry. A question that presupposes a "correct" answer encourages learners to look for absolutes. This kind of question is of dubious value particularly when the material invites questions of meaning rather than questions of fact. For example, an activity that directs a child to "cut and paste" reinforces the most obvious factual learning. Suggestions that children draw their interpretation of a biblical story encourage responses to the meaning of the narrative.

Some teachers say that they would not know the answers to open-ended questions. They are unsure of their own knowledge, and this feeling of ignorance leaves them vulnerable. Written directions in the manual to "Ask someone to look this up during the week," or "Ask your minister to come to class to answer questions" do not solve the problem for the teacher faced with an unanswerable question. Teachers feel equally uncertain with activity work that sets no standards for accomplishment. Perhaps the children will refuse to draw a picture. Teachers might try to direct a story dramatization only to find that discipline gets out of hand. The basic question here is what makes material "teachable."

There is no way to ensure attendance at teacher training conferences where teachers could learn new methods. Can any support be built into written material? One thinks of "how-to" articles in popular magazines in which instruction is given on how to accomplish astonishing projects, from mastering French cuisine to building a patio. People attempt such projects and some have the skills to succeed. Teachers are encouraged by seeing brief, inviting articles that will make them feel comfortable with open-ended questions or that provide step-by-step directions for story dramatizations that will give teachers confidence to try the method.

Theological interpretation and teaching methods need to be correlated. It would be unfortunate to use only simple methods that could defeat important goals. Clearly written materials and adequate support would help teachers expand their repertoire of skills. This requires funding at every level.

Toward an Ecumenical Curriculum

It was said earlier that the Uniform Lesson Series began as an interdenominational venture a century ago to be followed by the group-graded and closely graded lessons. Until the 1940s the group-graded outlines were shared by several denominations—Methodist, Congregational, and Presbyterian—but this consortium fell apart. The impetus for change came through denominational responses to neoorthodoxy and its approach to biblical interpretation.

Arising in Europe at the close of World War I, this theological approach found its most brilliant exponent in the Swiss pastor-turned-theologian Karl Barth and in the work of Emil Brunner. New biblical studies came from the research of Martin Dibelius and Rudolph Bultmann in Germany. Their work on form criticism added a new dimension to biblical studies that until that time had been involved in textual and literary criticism. Phrases such as "salvation history," "covenantal theology," and "book of the acts of God" were popularizations of a viewpoint that sought to interpret the Bible in its own setting and to refrain from a bias coming from the culture of the interpreter.

Neoorthodoxy was a reaction to the liberal theology popular in some Protestant circles at that time. Scorning such phrases as "the human search for God," it affirmed a biblical assertion that God is the initiator and humans have the choice of responding to or rejecting God's offer of redemption. Emphasis on the life and teachings of Jesus gave way to an emphasis on the event of the crucifixion-resurrection.

Slowly American schools of theology accepted this viewpoint. More slowly, the viewpoint informed the work of preaching. Eventually the viewpoint entered the consciousness of professionals in religious education. The first of the "new" materials was the *Christian Faith and Life* curriculum of the United Presbyterian Church (1948). This set that department of Christian education apart from those of the denominations with which it had cooperated until that time. Some denominations did not accept this biblical viewpoint in curriculum until new materials were introduced in the early 1960s.[3]

These curricula were intended to have limited life spans. It had been noticed that teachers grew tired of a curriculum after they had used it several times. Curricula on a two- or three-year cycle (meaning that a course would be rewritten or at least revised every two or three years) would have a probable life span of eight or nine years. Accordingly, a number of denominations teamed up to form the Joint Educational Development in 1968.[4] The curriculum enterprise had come full circle: There would again be an interdenominational curriculum.

This time, however, the fact of plurality was recognized. No longer could it be expected that one curriculum would be accepted by everyone. The theological atmosphere had broadened. The neoorthodox consensus, limited though it was, had ended.[5] Neoliberalism, neoevangelicalism, process theology, and liberation theology all had their advocates in the seminaries and through publishing houses. A theologically eclectic curriculum was a possibility.

A financial element also was involved. The cost of launching a new curriculum had risen drastically. No one body could afford the sum—not after the drastic curtailment of denominational budgets in the late 1960s. Financial need as much as anything drove denominations together to preserve a church-sponsored curriculum. There was also the hope of recapturing a larger percentage of their own constituencies from the independent publishers.

This was the origin of Christian Education: Shared Approaches, popularly known by the acronym CE:SA. The curriculum presents four options or approaches. Each approach is designed to meet the needs of a different constituency, although the designers recognized (less enthusiastically, however) that some parishes would want to mix the approaches. They would prefer that churches mix approaches only from one age level to another and not within a particular age level.

These four approaches will be described because they include the elements with which any curriculum will have to deal. Instead of omitting one element or trying to incorporate all into a single curriculum, the planners have provided the building blocks for a parish.

Knowing the Word is the most conservative in thought and methodologically is the simplest curriculum to use. It is broadly graded in the children's levels (preschool, grades one to three, four to six, seven to nine). It follows biblical themes, and each session begins with a biblical story that is later related to the personal lives of the learners. Youth and adult materials use the Uniform Lesson Series outlines.[6] The content and method seem close enough to materials published by independent houses to attract some of the smaller membership or more conservative churches who have rejected their denominations' earlier material. It is open in its approach to biblical interpretation.

Interpreting the Word is an approach that focuses on the interpretation of Scripture. In educational theory, it asserts that the first task is to teach the content of key biblical materials to children ages five to eleven. This will be recognized as the concrete-operational stage of cognitive development in Jean Piaget's system.[7] The "content" is the basic biblical message that God loves and saves people. This content uses stories of love and judgment, sin and redemption, covenant and grace. Learners, beginning with grades seven to nine, are taught the skills for interpretation, and units of study use blocks of biblical materials, a method that is continued through youth and adult materials. It will appeal to those who want a biblical base with an emphasis on interpretation as well as application.

Living the Word is the approach that combines life experience with biblical materials in the most open way. Sessions and units are frequently biblically oriented with biblical material linked to the experiences of learners. Some units are experience oriented even on the children's level. Biblical material becomes a resource to enable learners to understand the meaning of the Christian life. It is an attractive option for use with adolescents who prefer to begin study with their own experiences.

Doing the Word consists of materials published annually by Friendship Press, an arm of the National Council of Churches, and materials from other publishers that emphasize the Christian response to the world. Two themes a year focus on the Christian responsibility in an area of social concern at home and abroad.[8] Action-reflection methodology is employed so that the learner is involved immediately or vicariously in the situation. This is not a fifty-two weeks' curriculum but, rather, units of study that could be used during regular church school programs or as special emphases. It lends itself to intergenerational events and elective courses for young people and adults. These materials are designed to be on the cutting edge of the church's mission.

What assessment can be made of this new venture? The most significant factor in the enterprise is that so many denominations have been able to find enough biblical and theological affinity to cooperate on something as serious as educational materials for their members. Another factor is that these materials have appealed to some churches that had previously written off denominational curriculum as not being responsive to their needs. This would seem to indicate that offering options in curriculum materials is important.

Several questions remain for users. Will it be possible to continue using materials that are not always rewritten but only minimally revised on each cycle as is *Interpreting the Word?* Is the format of the materials, particularly *Knowing the Word*, attractive enough to be competitive with those of independent publishers? (Surveys have indicated that format is an important criterion for materials' selection among teachers.) Is each of the approaches distinctive and consistent in the relationship of content to method? (Some methods are appropriate to the teaching of facts, others to the development of interpretation.) Can teachers be given help through a planning guide in order to choose units of study as "building blocks" for a parish program? (The presently available guides are designed for structuring parish planning.)[9]

There is a further concern about incorporating distinctive denominational ethos. At present there is no provision to do so. There are a few points at which worship and history are taught, particularly in *Living the Word*, but there is little place for distinctive emphases in baptism, the meaning of church membership, the interpretation of the Lord's Supper, denominational heritage, and present outreach. Each denomination needs to prepare such materials, but teachers need help in finding a place for such additions. It has been suggested that a church order material only for three quarters a year, thus leaving thirteen sessions free to be used throughout the year in any way they are needed.

This possibility requires a flexible approach to units. Learning options would give planners freedom to choose the subject matter as well as methods. Customarily the focus has been only on options for methods and materials within a unit. Freedom to plan a year's work, a prospect that some teachers like and others fear, does not at present include space to consider parish life, liturgy, history, or outreach as alternative units.

The CE:SA curriculum is a breakthrough because it represents a broad attempt at interdenominational cooperation. It might point the way for large denominations to determine if they could design more flexible curricula. Cooperation among several smaller denominational groups is occurring. Several in the Wesleyan tradition jointly produce the Aldersgate curriculum. Two Lutheran groups produce individual curricula but have cooperated on special projects and plan a joint curriculum in the near future.

One conclusion can be drawn from these developments. The trend is toward curriculum tailored to meet individual parish needs. This makes preplanning essential so that intelligent choices will be made.

Other Curricular Options

Meanwhile independent Protestant publishers continue to produce total curriculum packages. This approach is helpful for churches who feel that skills and resources are not available for making choices among other available curricula. The materials are easy to use and require little, if any, advance preparation, although any material is improved by some thoughtful adaptation on the part of a teacher, and many teachers have the desire to do this. The material is attractive and usually less expensive than denominational material. Courses are continually rewritten so that the long-time teacher has a feeling of using a new course every year—a decided stimulus to volunteers. Interpretations are evangelical but with distinct differences.[10] There may be an effort to present biblical material without theological interpretation (which is not really possible), to leave theologizing to the churches, and to emphasize the application of the Bible for everyday life. The material does not require the loyalty of every-Sunday attendance on the part of a teacher because anyone present at the morning's adult class could substitute, especially when the biblical material, if based on the Uniform Lessons Series outlines, is the same for children, youth, and adults.

The Orthodox churches have been aware of developments in religious education and have developed materials to convey their distinctive ethos through materials that are similar to others in the format of teacher manuals and children's reading books.[11]

Some would say that Roman Catholic curriculum development today is akin to the "Babel" period in Protestant religious education. Their materials, all from private publishers, may have been produced under the auspices of monastic orders, school book publishers, or private companies. There has been a strong emphasis on the use of biblical materials, a real awareness of life-oriented materials, a lively approach to introducing children to liturgy, and a concern to relate Christian belief to social justice.

The *Come to the Father Series* (Paulist Press) was introduced into the United States from the original French edition produced in Canada. Emphasis was on the Bible as redemptive history. The theme has been modified but elements of the original intention remain. The various components of Scripture, tradition, and life are happily combined in the series called *Life, Love, Joy* produced by Silver Burdett Co. With the professional look of schoolbooks, carefully planned teacher manuals, and a wide variety of suggested resources, it is handsomely printed. The most widely used material is that of William H. Sadlier, Inc., which stays middle-of-the road. It is in a constant process of revision and is interpreted by field representatives who present helpful teacher training for parishes and communities. Benziger, Bruce & Glencoe, Inc. publishes another middle-of-the-road curriculum. Winston Press, Inc. publishes several options designed for Protestants and Roman Catholics and publishes programs in moral development.

These materials are usually available for grades one through twelve, although some publishers produce distinctive courses of study for adolescents. Adult materials are produced independently of this basic curriculum.

Not having the long-time stereotypes that have sometimes inhibited creative change among adult classes in Protestant churches, Catholic parishes are free to develop new forms of adult education, using various media, and publishers are responding. Roman Catholic publishers have produced few preschool materials until recently. They have inherited a tradition that religious education was basically knowledge-oriented, and grade one has seemed an appropriate time to begin. The family attended Sunday Mass together and religious education classes were held during the week. Catholics have not had the need that Protestants had to provide classes for the whole family during the Sunday church school hour or classes for preschoolers while parents attended a church service. However, the development of preschool materials is increasing with several available now that relate faith to the experience of children.

Catholic materials are usually closely graded because parishes are large and, except in some rural areas, every grade will have a big enrollment. Increasingly, materials are being oriented to the untrained teacher. The sisters who used to teach parochial school and CCD classes are fewer in number, and their vocational options have broadened. In religious education they are likely to be parish coordinators, helping lay volunteers to teach. This confronts parishes with the same kinds of problems that Protestants have struggled with for nearly two centuries, and parish leaders are aware of this fact.

Catholic publishers also face questions about the relationship between biblical/theological material and life-oriented teaching. They struggle to win acceptance for materials that give teachers more freedom to plan. They have a stronger sense than have Protestant curriculum editors of the need to incorporate preparation for worship and reflection upon it into every year's study. They have a sense of church heritage, lacking in Protestant curriculum. Familiarity with Roman Catholic materials is essential for any broad understanding of the cutting edge of religious education curriculum today.

Materials produced by both the Southern Baptist Sunday School Board and by the United Methodist Church reach as many people as do all the CE:SA materials. Recognizing the desire of volunteer teachers for easy-to-use materials, these denominations have still encouraged some initiative by the teacher in enriching session plans. Both denominations begin with a biblically based curriculum from which life-experience applications flow. Neither gives many options at the children's level, but both have a wealth of materials for young people and adults. Each uses a three-year grading cycle except on the preschool level.

The Lutherans, with their strong liturgical tradition, have needs that the ecumenical Protestant curriculum cannot adequately meet. They also have a theological diversity that has made it necessary to produce several curricula, although as was noted earlier, they work together on special projects. The Lutheran Church in America materials provide a diversity of units within each age level and encourage parishes to plan accordingly. This means that a total curriculum could be correlated around one theme for a year. Or a specific class could choose a different theme each quarter—biblical, experiential, or church-oriented. Flexibility is encouraged. The American Lutheran Church, more evangelically oriented, has frequently begun with biblical materials and applied these to children's experience. The Missouri Synod (Concordia Publishing House) teaches a fundamentalist approach to the Bible through materials that are attractively developed with an interesting use of media.

Such a brief overview hardly does justice to the diversity of materials available. Only an examination of curricula can indicate the distinctiveness of each. It becomes certain, however, that while a diversity of needs may be met, parishes will need to do serious thinking about their own goals, their theological and educational presuppositions, and the amount of effort that they are willing and able to expend for the teaching task.

Chapter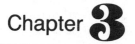

People Involved in Curriculum

The teacher who uses a course of study seldom realizes how many people were involved in its production. The writer's name rarely is recognized. The list of editors holds no meaning. Yet these people have determined the shape of the material to be taught. The influences they exert raise issues for curriculum development.

People at the Source

The source of denominational curriculum planning lies in people at the top echelons of a central office. Trained professionally in religious education and theology, they bring viewpoints that will significantly affect the written curriculum. Theologically they will represent their denomination's viewpoint, that is, the viewpoint most widely held among the constituency. The editors of independent companies, Protestant and Roman Catholic, will represent the viewpoints held by their constituency.

Customarily, planning for the development of denominational curriculum involves the thinking of both the department of religious education and the publication department, although editorial authority lies with the latter, as was indicated in the previous chapter. The foundation papers from Joint Educational Development represented the thinking of the constituent denominations for the CE:SA materials.[1] The principles on which a curriculum will be built are developed at this level. This work determines the basic biblical and theological stance, the understanding of Christian living and outreach, and the relationship of content to experience-oriented materials. These leaders also settle upon basic educational principles, determining in general the approach they think will be most suitable for conveying the content at each age level. Basic goals are established.

A series of position papers may be circulated to summarize the results of this process or to familiarize people with the basic content.[2] Any research for curriculum planning in a congregation needs to include a study of such sources. The final form of the curriculum will indicate both a concurrence with and some modification of the original conception.

Key persons in curriculum writing (as distinguished from preparatory development) are the editors. Although the editor-in-chief has responsibility for the entire project, in practice the form that materials take reflects the work done by age-level editors who divide responsibilities for preschool children, elementary age, youth, and adults. Each of these editors may have a staff who develop materials for particular levels within the larger grouping. Editors usually will have theological and/or religious education backgrounds, and editors of children's materials frequently have a background in general education. Some have had training in writing and/or editing, but others are trained on the job. The editor has a complex job to do. The established presuppositions for the curriculum must always be kept in mind while evaluating manuscripts.

In addition, editors must have some knowledge about the age group for which the writing will be done: the learning potential and limitations of those learners as well as their needs, concerns, and interests. Such information will be basic to their critique of the material written for pupils and the material written for teachers. When materials for children's classes are under consideration, the editor needs to be able to find and use a style that will capture the interest of the child and a style that a teacher will find to be clear. Each piece of material serves a different function. Editors spend much of their time analyzing, correcting, and even rewriting material submitted to them by assigned writers. They also do the more mundane tasks of keeping in touch with writers to be sure that various deadlines are met for outlines, first drafts, completed manuscripts, and revisions.

Writers are the persons in the most direct contact with the users of curriculum because their writing is the substance that the teacher uses. No amount of editing will make a weak manuscript strong. Words may be changed, sentence constructions simplified, descriptions of and directions for activities clarified, but the result will still be a made-over job. Some people have developed a skill for writing curricular materials. Some can write a teacher's manual, which is addressed to adults, but cannot write children's material because this requires a different style. Some writers have a skill for developing a workbook with imaginative learning exercises but cannot write a vivid story. Some can produce excellent expository material for adult readers but do not know how to develop a teaching plan so that a volunteer teacher can easily follow the steps from the beginning of a session to its end.

Unfortunately, the people who write these materials are not uniformly competent. One can look at the author's name in the front of a particular course of study and know that the material will be well written, imaginative, and yet practical, because this person has had experience in curriculum writing. Others clearly have not developed this skill. Editors select writers, and the final responsibility devolves upon them. Perhaps there are not enough competent writers in this field to do the work needed. Sometimes editors, who have plenty of problems with late manuscripts, continue to employ some writers because they meet deadlines faithfully even though their work may need rewriting. The fact remains that curriculum material is uneven in quality. This causes some teachers to reject a course book as unteachable and to disparage the whole curriculum.

Independent publishers seem to fare better. They require a uniform style that assures a commendable degree of writing competence. All editors face a decision as to whether to encourage personal style (sometimes called creativity) or to follow the model of popular magazines and require a uniform style. Because the users of curriculum materials are also people who read popular magazines, the uniform style may make materials easier to use.

Curriculum writers are not usually specially trained for their jobs. Some writing workshops are available, but attendance is not a prerequisite for an assignment. Some editors have the custom of scheduling individual conferences with writers. This assures the writer of knowing the editor's expectations, but limits the possibility of the writer's feeling involved in a total curriculum project. At the height of its curriculum development, the United Presbyterian Church used to hold three-day writers' conferences. Plenary sessions were addressed by theological resource persons; age-level groups worked together on planning; and individual conferences between editors and writers completed the work. The interaction among writers and editors developed a sense of purpose, a commitment to the task, and a fund of ideas.

Liaison People

The next people who deal with the curriculum are the field persons who mediate between the national office where the material is produced and the parishes in which it is used. These are the people sent out to introduce the curriculum and later to service it. They meet with teachers and religious education committees, show how to use the materials, hear about problems, and train teachers in more effective ways of teaching. Some publishers of Roman Catholic materials employ staff persons who work in particular geographical areas as consultants. The Southern Baptist Convention has such a staff who gather annually at the Nashville headquarters for a conference that includes the editorial and publishing staff. Many denominations no longer send out field representatives from the national office because this responsibility has been given to the judicatory as a "grass roots" operation, thought to be closer to local church needs. Independent publishers employ regional representatives as well as having "troubleshooters" at headquarters.

The task of interpretation usually falls on a person on a judicatory staff who may have a background in religious education. This may be one of several portfolios held by the person unless there is a large staff that includes someone specifically skilled in the area of children's work or work with young people. Responsibilities may include the planning of conferences for people of all ages. Frequently this staff person is also designated "area minister" and may have oversight of one geographical section of the judicatory. Area ministers are available upon invitation to come into parishes to help plan for curricular needs, to help choose and implement materials. The system is only as useful as the capabilities of the resource persons, the rapport they are able to establish with lay workers in the parish, and the willingness of the latter to learn how to use materials. Frequently teachers will blame problems on the material itself and change to those from another publisher.

The interpretative task can also be accomplished by teacher training, but it would be unrealistic to say that this has been effective. Judicatories set up such conferences only to find that teachers will not go as far as the next town in order to spend a day in training. Even the teachers of one denomination within a community seldom engage in joint leadership education, profitable as this might be. A once-flourishing program of interdenominational community training schools has long since vanished without replacement.

Yet, as the Joint Educational Development people point out, parish religious education is a total system. If any part is missing, the whole will be weakened. Teacher development and support are components of the system. It is a question whether any curriculum can be taught effectively without these elements. Surely, no program that depends on the use of a variety of skills by untrained teachers can be used successfully unless these teachers seek and receive help.

People in the Parish

The third group of people involved in the curriculum are those in the local congregation. At the head of this structure is the pastor, although the nature of authority held by the pastor varies from one denomination to another. Sometimes the pastor's annual report to the denomination includes a listing of curriculum materials being used. In other parishes, the minister would have to search through cabinets to discover what each teacher is using. The pastor both represents and reinforces the theological climate of a parish. The pastor also influences the status of religious education by the degree of personal concern expressed and the willingness to be involved in the program at specific points. Usually pastors are involved in overall curriculum planning and in the choice of materials—although some teachers will later make personal substitutions unknown to anyone outside the class.

The governing board comes in contact with the curriculum at the point of the budget. In small churches, teaching materials may be the largest item of religious education expenditures. Committees sometimes wonder at the cost and question if so many pieces of writing are necessary. Materials may include a teacher manual, pupil book, resource packet, pupil workbook, take-home papers, and other items. Little money may be left over for other materials and activities. Members of the board need to be kept informed about the purposes and uses of the materials and the reasons for the choices made. Their cooperation is important.

The religious education committee should be the body directly responsible for the choice of curriculum. The words "should be" are used advisedly. Many committees do not exercise this responsibility, preferring to leave the choice to each teacher. Teachers are difficult to recruit, and anything that would make a teacher content is usally acceptable. Such an attitude is unfortunate because the religious education committee is the key to effective educational work in a parish. It has responsibility for planning a total program. Selecting teaching materials is one aspect of its task. This selection is where the curriculum planning materials mentioned earlier would be useful. Whether such planning is accomplished in one committee session or extended through a year of study, the process would be an education in itself for both the committee members and teachers.

A traditional Sunday church school is headed by a superintendent whose task is primarily administrative. This person takes responsibility for ordering and distributing material and for listening to teachers' problems. Few consider it necessary to become familiar with the material. The persons who are most likely to study the material in some depth are departmental superintendents in large membership churches. These people may have some background in education to be both resource persons and administrators. Only the coordinator or director of religious education, usually a professionally trained person, could be expected to have knowledge of both the theory and content of a curriculum. The parish large enough to be able to afford the services of such a person can offer knowledgeable support to teachers at all times.

The final decision as to whether curriculum materials are adequate is made by the teachers. Judicatory heads, curriculum publishers, and editors are all aware of this fact. Teachers frequently determine what material will be taught and how it will be taught, abandoning suggested methods and materials at will and interpreting texts from a personal viewpoint. The last is inevitable, for people view materials through their own perceptions, and communication between writer and teacher can never be complete. The teacher's approach also determines the response of the learner to the material—"I don't like that stuff," "I can't draw pictures," "That story is dull"—or, conversely, entices the learner to explore the material and enjoy the satisfactions of learning. Admittedly some pupils come well-disposed to enjoy the session, and others arrive reluctantly and/or intermittently. Such factors influence pupil response to materials. In

addition teachers may choose to use or ignore suggested resources that could enrich learning. Some are hesitant to go
beyond a basic outline; others do not find or take time to look
for materials, and others are in churches that cannot afford to
procure resources or are located where these are not readily
available.

One other group has some influence on the choice of curriculum materials: the parents of young learners. Parents will affirm
that they want their children to "learn the Bible," but they rarely
clarify what they mean. Nor do planners in parish education
help them to be specific. However, this affirmation of faith in
the efficacy of Bible teaching is widely influential in churches.
Parents may also have doubts about issue-oriented curricular
materials used with adolescents. Young people, too, will exercise
a veto over material used in their classes either by passive re-
sistance or by their absence. Adults choose their own curriculum, and their preferences determine both the number of classes
made available and the size of a group.

Bridging the Gap

A vast array of people are involved in the curriculum process.
These range from highly trained staff members to untrained and
faithful believers. All have similar goals. Yet frequently the parish volunteers feel that their wishes are not being heard, while
the staff people feel that no one really understands what they
are trying to do. This raises a basic question: what should be
the relationship of principle to practice? Can and should editors
try to persuade people in parishes to accept their premises? Are
they sensitive to the needs of lay teachers?

There are no easy answers and no final answers. If the premises held seem to be at either end of a continuum, then it is
difficult to know how far each group can move toward understanding the other. Editors are vulnerable at the point of being
paid representatives of the church. They need not try to meet
every criticism, but local churches can vote with their pocketbook
by taking their business elsewhere. The kinds of options made
available in CE:SA indicate concern by a number of denominations to serve a wide variety of needs. Eventually parishes
also need to indicate some willingness to grapple with serious
issues and reflect critically on their educational needs.

Communication between national offices and local churches
could bring some mutual understanding of what each is trying

to accomplish. Staff people also are involved in the life of local parishes and have that perspective. Parish people may be less personally acquainted with national staff. Few people live near enough to central headquarters to be able to visit, but other ways could be found of being introduced to each other. One independent publisher offers to set up telephone conferences.[3] The group of teachers at one end of the line has read preparatory material. After that, hearing the voices while looking at a photo of the team at the other end of the line develops empathy between publisher and user. The United Methodist Church has maintained an "800" telephone number through which a staff member can give information and interpretation to inquirers.

Related to sensitivity to local needs is the question of the kind of evaluation that needs to be made of curriculum materials. As was pointed out earlier, independent publishers, needing to show a profit, take the "bottom-line" figures as the final criterion. If the material isn't selling, it is not meeting needs. Such material must be revised, rewritten, restructured, or dropped. Denominations have guidelines for evaluating the effectiveness of their work. They make surveys from churches, judicatories, and seminaries to elicit response to the educational and theological goals of the curriculum. Such surveys may uncover to what extent the goals of the planners have been met, but sales are a more likely indication of buyer satisfaction. Questionnaires sent to parishes asking how their needs are being met could provide some indication of *their* goals. This type of testing would indicate to the developers any disparity between their own curriculum goals and the expressed needs of the users.

In asking to what extent local needs and desires should be met, one is also asking the question of how important volume sales should be. Sales represent an affirmation by the constituency, but they are also necessary for a viable business venture. It may be questioned whether denominations should subsidize materials that their people do not want to buy, however excellent those materials might be.

People are working at the national level to improve curriculum materials. At the same time, people work at the local scene with the weekly concern to find enough teachers for every class session. Their practical solution is to choose materials that anyone can follow easily with little or no preparation. With such help, almost anyone could become a last-minute substitute. The goal of obtaining easily teachable materials will affect both the content and the methods of a course. There would be no time to assemble enrichment materials and no time to substitute one activity for another, and so the session plans must be self-contained and easily outlined.

Teacher training would seem to be an answer, but the response is made from the local church that it is difficult enough to *find* teachers for each class without hoping to train them. Everyone knows that choir members attend a weekly practice evening and seem to become a cohesive group through such training. Why are many teachers unwilling to be similarly prepared for their work? Sometimes the need for planning a unit of teaching will encourage teachers to meet together, and team teaching almost necessitates such planning. But most teachers go to their respective classes week after week as if they were not part of a larger enterprise.

In many black churches it is the practice for the minister to meet weekly or biweekly with Sunday church school teachers to study the biblical material where everyone uses the Uniform Lessons Series. The problem of teacher training affects CCD teachers less because their large parishes usually have a trained coordinator who can meet individually and in small groups with teachers. Many dioceses offer courses on both content and method, awarding certificates for the successful completion of basic study.

The key person in most parishes is the pastor, the one person with some presumed theological, biblical, and—perhaps—religious education background. Little effort is made to assist clergy in their educational task. If they simply shared in biblical inquiry with teachers, studied with them about the worship of the church, or explained the meaning of faith and belief, this would stimulate the thinking of teachers who might then develop teaching methods to communicate their own learning to their pupils. The task could involve enlisting the talents of parishioners in public or private school teaching as resource persons who would share their skills with volunteer teachers. An informed teacher is eager to share new insights. Any curriculum material will be enriched as a teacher's own understanding is deepened.

Teachers find it useful to have materials that include with each session an abbreviated outline that could be used for emergencies. Suggestions could also be given for alternatives. "When the Teacher Is Absent" might be a section of each session plan that suggests specific procedures such as story reading, film, or filmstrip resources, a sharing of historical remembrances of the parish by a longtime member, or an explanation by a member of one of the boards or groups of its work. Suggestions could be made of ways to integrate one class into another as visitors. No one has yet put imagination to work to see how the value of serious teaching as a task can be maintained while the legitimate need for using substitute teachers is met.

The Theological Factor in Curriculum Discussion

The margin of difference between the expectations of those at the top level of curriculum planning and those who carry out the teaching at the local level is one critical factor in the development and acceptance of materials. Another factor is the discrepancy in expectations as to how much training and preparation should be expected in order to use a curriculum effectively. A third difference is in the area of theology.

The basic American religious ethos is orthodox, evangelical, moralistic, and pietistic. Descriptively this means that many people accept biblical records at face value, and if they have any doubts, they will allow some leeway for explanation but prefer to leave more complicated questions unexplored. Many have strong doctrinal positions. People hold, theoretically at least, to a moral code based on the Ten Commandments and the Golden Rule. They also believe in a direct relationship to God through personal prayer, a factor that takes precedence over the worship of the congregation. Many people are not concerned about theologizing, that is, exploring the meaning of doctrines such as atonement, incarnation, or the Trinity. They want simple explanations for their beliefs.

While they might seem to be uninterested in theology, to assume this would be a mistake. Believers of every persuasion can sense when teaching materials are not expressing their personal theological premises. On a common-sense level they will reject one course of study and choose another because it "sounds right." One person explained this attitude as "if it doesn't say 'Jesus loves you' in simple terms, it is not being theologically correct." Now there are many ways of affirming this theological statement, most of them not so explicitly. The "simple" believing teacher needs to have it stated explicitly. The planners of many curricula prefer to phrase the affirmation in more formal theological terms. Or, one could say that many teachers insist on pious language. The material must sound religious on every page. In the thinking of curriculum planners, material may be religious without using religious words. This stance is difficult to explain to teachers who insist that lessons begin with biblical material. They are uncomfortable with interpretative materials for teacher or pupil that present critical inquiry of the biblical text, form, or structure.

Teachers "feel" what they miss in some teaching materials although they might not give this feeling concrete expression. When they say that they want more Bible, they might mean that they want less biblical interpretation and more straightforward answers. When they say that the material is not spiritual enough, they may mean that they miss particular language that sounds spiritual to them. When they say that the material isn't really Christian, they may find an emphasis on doctrine (such as "Christ died for your sins") lacking or be uncomfortable with broad moral choices that seem to be offered to pupils.

They find such needs met in materials by publishers who never fail to phrase their writings in the familiar religious words that make their constituencies comfortable. Remembering the extent of evangelical feeling within "main line" Protestant churches, it should not be surprising that numbers of Sunday church school teachers choose such materials. Roman Catholic constituencies have similar needs. They, too, are serviced by publishers across the theological/biblical spectrum, the language of whose material brings familiar imagery to mind and assures users that they are teaching the "true faith."

The question is how denominational publishers should meet this conflict between the theological assumptions and approach demanded by some of their constituents. None of the large denominations, except the Southern Baptists, has broad theological consistency among its parishes. Denominations that do, usually smaller religious groups, have fewer problems gaining acceptance for an official curriculum. What the publication departments of many denominations desire is to encourage the freedom to interpret biblical and theological insights. They may accept the classical creeds and have historical interpretative material, like the Westminster, Augsburg, and Heidelburg confessions or the Baltimore catechism, but they do not want learners taught that there is only one way of viewing the Bible or only one interpretation of basic Christian doctrines. They try to structure this freedom of inquiry into the materials. Many clergy and teachers prefer the security of a specific biblical interpretation.

The editors' approach is "liberal" not for what it says about God or Jesus but because of the way it tries to encourage parents and teachers to explore the meaning of God and Jesus.

There is no easy solution. The basis for theological inquiry could be written into the introductory teacher materials, although many teachers skip these pages and turn immediately to the outlines for teaching. Perhaps it might be written into specific session plans. For example: "Some Christians affirm that . . ." followed by an explanation as to why this is accepted as truth. Then "We affirm the statement, too, but want you as growing Christians under the guidance of the Holy Spirit to think about how it is true for you, how it has been true through the church's past, and how the meaning of the statement can be expressed for today." Teaching materials need also to leave space for both teachers and learners to deal with doubt.

Decision making is an integral part of being and becoming a Christian. Clergy, as the trained theologians within a congregation, should be able to enable teachers to wrestle with such a statement both for themselves and for their pupils. Beyond that, educational planners will need to accept the fact that not all of their people believe with the same openness to inquiry and that not all materials will be useful for everyone.

Chapter 4

Planning in the Congregation

It is a truism to say that no two churches are alike. Publishers try to keep this fact in mind when they develop curriculum materials, but facing its implications is a difficult task. Some adaptations can be suggested for the varieties of situations, but frequently people who teach in parishes are not adept at making changes. Wise editors structure such suggestions into the written material: for example, how to adapt group-graded material to a closely graded situation, or closely graded materials to classes that include children across a broad age span; what minimal material to use with intermittent attenders; and how to enrich the sessions for the regulars. Without such specific help, there is a high risk that the material will be rejected as impractical. The usual statement is "We can't use it in our situation," or "I can't teach this." Local church planners need also to be aware of these factors.

Information That Helps

In order to lessen the possibility of such response, curriculum planners could draw on a wealth of material at their immediate command. There are statistics on church membership and Sunday church school enrollment, usually by age groups. They may know the number of people teaching, the material being used, and the age distribution within churches. In addition, the publication department knows where materials are sold and from this information can have an idea of the size and sociological complexion of communities, whether in city, town, or rural areas. From such material could be compiled pertinent facts for writers, with suggestions as to how this information should affect the writing.

A large enrollment for religious education will make possible more class options and, frequently, more potential teachers because the parish can draw from a larger pool of recruits. The large church may have a broad sociological and educational distribution among members, indicating more variety in teaching skills. Large enrollments also indicate that there will be more classes, larger enrollments in each class, and perhaps a closely graded arrangement for children. In contrast, if the material is selling to many small churches, this indicates that group-graded or even broadly graded materials will be needed. The sales figures indicate the constituency. Nonrenewals may indicate lost constituencies that could be reclaimed.

Age-distribution figures point to areas that need special development. In years after an upswing in the birth rate, there will be a large number of young children. When there appears to be a trend toward increased adult attendance, then serious attention should be given to programs for adults. The present interest in analyzing stages in adult life[1] suggests that this factor might have an effect on the direction taken by new materials.

Geographical setting is a factor that indicates not only the possible size of parish constituencies but also their concerns. There is a rich variety of life-styles among people in different areas of the land, from New England to California. The same can be said for Canadian life-styles from Newfoundland to Vancouver Island. There are differences of life-styles in the British Isles and the broad spaces of Australia and New Zealand. To what extent will these factors influence curriculum development? No single curriculum can appeal to such diversity, but writers can become sufficiently aware of educational, cultural, vocational, and economic differences to meet the needs of potential users.

Not all such information will directly affect a course of study. Sensitivity to sociological factors can be included in the introductory material and be picked up within specific session plans in the form of questions and suggestions. Guided questions are needed, such as "What in your community life might have some parallel to the biblical situation of . . .?" or "Remembering what is going on in your parish, how does this biblical passage speak to . . .? Alert both writer and teacher to the impact of the immediate situation. The writer does not try to anticipate every contingency. The teacher is being taught and encouraged to become aware of factors that can both enrich and individualize the teaching. This interaction between the people at each end of the curriculum production process is essential if the teaching materials are to be dynamic and individual.

Factors in Community Life

There are specific factors about which editors do not have information but which parish leaders must consider in selecting materials. This information is available for those who intentionally gather facts. They need to know how many potential learners there are at each age level through adolescence. This will indicate the number of classes and the size of each—helpful information not only for ordering supplies but also for assigning space.[2]

Local church planners need to know the composition of potential adult groups: educational and professional backgrounds of the adults, for example. Such information will indicate the skills, orientations, and needs of learners. It will suggest some idea of the styles of teaching to which these people are accustomed and the preparation that would be needed to win their acceptance of changes. Further questions will elicit interests, times available for participation, and approximate age levels. Such knowledge of a constituency may be gleaned from questionnaires, telephone conversations, or individual interviews. As a practical detail, a higher percentage of returns from questionnaires can be expected when a number of people are gathered together to write this information instead of being sent the questionnaires by mail.

Some adult groups are formed on the basis of individual initiative, primarily for mutual support, and the material they choose to study may be directly related to that fact: psychological or spiritual reading or personally oriented study groups. Some groups form for social needs—"fellowship." These would usually be people of similar interests, and the materials might vary from child study to preparing for retirement. Some may wish to engage in critical exploration of biblical or theological material. Others may be concerned with issues of personal religious living, social justice, or the outreach of the church. The needs and interests of adults are so varied as to make mass-produced materials virtually impossible. Short-term courses are a necessity. Inquiry into these needs is a clue to choosing materials, and awareness of sales figures is a clue to publishers as to current interests among adults.

The next circle of concern is the community itself. People bring their whole lives into the orbit of the church. Although the producers of curriculum can know only general demographic statistics, each parish can gather information about its own community. The methods used to teach children and adolescents in public schools will affect the range of teaching approaches possible in the church. For example, learning centers were established in schools years before the ideas were incorporated into religious education curriculum. Church teachers not already exposed to the idea will need training in order to use such new techniques.

Where there is unemployment in a community, this factor will affect both adults and children. It may appear in the classroom in the form of a child's anxiety and a vague feeling of insecurity. It may trigger in adolescents an indifference to exploring vocational options. Adults may ask what the Christian faith can have to say in a complex economic situation where people have been taught that work is the very essence of existence and then have been denied the possibility of secure employment.

Other aspects of community life also impinge on a church's educational program. Poverty is endemic in rural areas as well as in large cities. In addition to producing specific courses on world hunger, curriculum developers need to structure illustrative material from social concerns into regular units of study. Teachers, through the introductory material in the teaching manual, could be advised to list for themselves basic community concerns that might affect the teaching of a course.

Parish planners need to know something about the athletic and cultural opportunities available in the community and area. This information will suggest possibilities for curriculum enrichment: group attendance at a sports event, a visit to a museum to see artifacts from biblical times or to view religious art; group attendance at a film or play that is pertinent to a unit of study or a congregational concern. A long community tradition of music will be reflected in churches with active choirs. Such churches rarely find available units of study on hymns and other religious music for any age level.[3]

An understanding of the work carried on in the community is another factor for knowledgeable curriculum building. Rural communities have special values and skills, but sometimes one gets the impression that curriculum materials, based as they are frequently on farm-oriented biblical imagery, ignore the fact that the Bible also addresses people who live in cities. A knowledge of factory and marketplace, research laboratory and university, adds information for the people who use curriculum.

Any community includes many religious groups, most of which operate independently of one another. Even those within a single confessional group seldom cooperate as effectively as they might. A knowledge of other churches might uncover the information that they are using the same or similar teaching materials and that more effective teacher preparation might be accomplished by working together. Knowledge of other religious groups would provide opportunities for high school and adult classes to exchange visits to learn about the symbolism of the building, liturgy, and beliefs. Clergy and knowledgeable laity could introduce visiting groups to their tradition. There is no better way to learn about one's own tradition than to have to explain it to someone else.

If ecumenicity is to become more than a little-understood word, the practice of interchurch cooperation will need to start where people have an acquaintance with one another. Yet people who have known one another socially for years have rarely visited one another's churches except for a wedding or funeral. When interchange occurs, it is more frequently among clergy. Some churches have become knowledgeable about ways they can work together to share faith and serve the community. Ventures in ecumenical Bible study are not uncommon, but they usually begin through the initiative of a few people, laity or clergy. The few materials available for ecumenical study and action are offered through the national offices concerned with this dimension of church life and are not usually listed in the curriculum catalogue. This points to the limited focus of most curriculum catalogues.

The ecumenical approach can be structured into other curriculum units. To their credit, the planners of the CE:SA materials have issued a curriculum evaluation sheet that asks about the ecumenical dimension in courses of study. A rough perusal of those materials, however, suggests that even here the concern is hardly in the forefront of the editors' consciousness. In the church situation today, ecumenicity is not something to be talked about or studied but something to be lived. The most realistic involvement would be through interparish activity by means of joint study groups, worship, and such educational ventures as vacation church schools, retreats, and conferences.

Regional concerns should be another focus for curriculum planning, especially at the local level. People in the states that lie within the region known as Appalachia need to be concerned about the needs of people there, asking how they as companion churches can become involved. Study materials may be generated at the national level, but the specific application must come from those who live near the region. Churches in cities need to be aware of the needs of companion congregations in rural areas, and the reverse is also true. Vacation experiences are a potential source of learning. Teachers usually ask the class on the first fall Sunday: "Where did you go this summer? What did you do?" The experience of participating in Christian community could be deepened by considering in advance churches to visit and ways to meet people.

Summer is a time for inquiring into the meaning of leisure and recreation. Why do some people feel good and others feel guilty about using leisure time? Many young people engage in work and study projects at home or abroad during the summer. Preparatory materials before starting the venture and reflection on their activities after their return could increase the effectiveness of the learning experience. Information about the availability of such projects may originate at the national or judicatory level, but some are planned by parishes. A general planning guidebook would be a helpful curriculum tool.

Statistics and Curriculum Choice

Attendance patterns affect the kind of curricular materials that can be used. Most courses of study assume regular class attendance, yet attendance records in local churches do not bear out this confident assumption. In some areas, the weekend away is a tradition. Elsewhere people have other reasons for sporadic attendance. This situation requires materials that do not build from one session to the next but are self-contained weekly experiences. The alternative would be careful attention to review for returned class members. Some churches would find it more effective to hold weekday classes, and they structure curriculum materials accordingly.

People are not noted for lifelong denominational loyalty. It is important to know the religious backgrounds of constituents because this will influence their approaches to biblical interpretation as teachers and learners. Some have chosen their present church affiliation either in reaction against a previous one or as a positive response to a new direction in their own thinking, whether liberal or conservative. The theological/biblical orientation of those who work professionally in the church—clergy, organist/choir director, and religious education leaders—will be determinative in the choice of materials for worship, preaching, and teaching enrichment.

There needs to be some consensus on the interpretation of the Christian faith that people are learning through the worship service and what they are learning in a class setting. Contradictions at this point could be one reason why teachers want to choose their own materials. Some may not be comfortable with what they hear in the Sunday service and want to promote a more acceptable viewpoint through teaching. Thus it not infrequently happens that what is being taught in religious education classes may be a biblically conservative interpretation while at the worship service, hymns and sermon reflect a liberal view. If both messages are really being heard, this disparity could cause some confusion, if not conflict. Curriculum planners need to inquire into the theological presuppositions of a parish—both clergy and laity—before choosing materials.

This is not the only area in which information about the makeup of the parish is essential to wise curriculum planning. It is important to know the number of children at different age levels in order to assess whether closely graded, group-graded or broadly graded materials are most useful. There is an age span beyond which closely graded materials are not functional. In a group of children that included grades one to three it would be as difficult to adapt grade one material to meet the concerns and capabilities of third graders as it would be to adapt third grade material to children just entering the first grade. The converse is also true: if there is a large number of children in one grade, the selectivity made possible by closely graded materials will be needed in order to make individual adaptations within the variations among children of any one age.

Statistics about the educational and vocational composition of the parish will be helpful in deciding the kind of teaching manuals needed. Highly educated people and others of creative bent do not want to be confined by too specific a teaching outline. They need material that offers the freedom to plan and encourages them to use extra resources. Such leaders would feel tied down by step-by-step plans in a self-contained session outline. On the other hand, some very able people would like to teach but do not feel secure about planning. Other people do not want to spend much time in preparation. These will need carefully outlined materials unless there is a well-qualified coordinator or department superintendent who can help them plan the sessions.

Pupil materials also need to fit the needs of learners in a particular setting. A children's class requires books on several reading levels in addition to the basic pupil material. Children who read quickly will be bored by having material beneath their reading level while others will struggle to find meaning in any storybook. Activity books that seem trivial to some children, especially if the technique is familiar from school, may provide absorbing exercises for other children. Some children are so saturated by the media approach at school that projected visual materials hold little interest. This emphasizes the fact that methods are simply tools to clarify and enrich learning.

The kinds of media used in schools daily affect the skills children bring to the church. Many who are accustomed at school to reading a book silently in order to answer questions of meaning, arrive at a religious education class only to find that the teacher asks the class to read a story aloud, each child taking a turn. Some have finished reading the story silently before the oral reading is halfway through. Again, children are introduced to research tools early in their school experience as they use dictionaries and encyclopedias. Similar resource books could be made available for Bible study at children's level, but few religious education classes take advantage of this skill in order to enrich Bible study.

Thought-provoking material is needed for people who are used to inquiry and not afraid to question basic assumptions. Such people would be impatient with materials that seem to deny their intelligence by uncritical statements. Both adolescents and adults need mind-stretching courses of study. Teaching manuals for children's teachers should also provide stimulating introductory material about both biblical backgrounds and teaching approaches. It is important to remember that teachers are learning as they teach.

On the other hand some people are looking for affirmation. They want answers, and they look for an authoritative approach from the teaching material to strengthen their faith. Studies that raise questions rather than provide answers would be rejected. Forward-looking religious educators may be disturbed by this attitude, but people feel free to explore meanings only from a personal sense of security. Such persons can be prepared for a more flexible approach by a thoughtful, encouraging teacher (or teaching manual) who affirms the belief structure of a class before asking members to give reasons for their faith. An openness to new meaning is worth cultivating as a goal for learners. This will help them become tolerant of viewpoints other than their own. Teaching materials cannot be so structured as to achieve this goal. An inquiring attitude is developed through thoughtful interaction among clergy and laity within the Christian community.

The biblical and theological presuppositions of curriculum materials need to be consonant with those of the particular religious tradition, the people of the parish, and the pastor. People assume that denominational material will reflect a tradition, but the variations from liberal to conservative among parishes within a tradition is so wide that there is no such guarantee that the material will fit the needs of a given parish. For this reason independent publishers may (or, conversely, may not) better reflect local viewpoints. Similar diversity may be found among the numerous publishers of Roman Catholic materials.

Methods for teaching material should also conform to the needs and capabilities of the users. A teacher who is willing to plan ahead will probably also be open to the use of a variety of teaching methods. The methods with which children are familiar through school define both the potential and the limitations of usable methods for religious education. Some adults have long been accustomed to having class leaders who lecture or who comment on the material printed in the study book. Some people prefer to participate in small discussion groups while others enjoy a presentation followed by a question period.

The makeup of the parish will suggest preferred styles of teaching. Churches that have remained stable in membership for many years tend to be conservative in their religious education structure. Larger churches, especially in suburban communities, may include a number of persons whose everyday work involves them in many learning approaches. They are accustomed to the process of problem solving. The large membership church has an advantage in being able to offer groups that meet diverse needs, both in content and method. Small churches can plan some variety in learning opportunities through the use of short-term units and through groups that meet at times other than Sunday morning. In this way, the existence of the traditional type of Bible class is not threatened by something new.

Global Aspects of Curriculum

One other factor to be included in curriculum development is that of social justice on a global scale. Presently, in addition to the concern about poverty noted earlier, the concern about environment has high priority, along with issues of war, peace, and the balance of armaments. This information comes even to children through daily television but is rarely structured into curriculum materials. There are excellent adult and high school courses, but the regular curricular materials are so tightly structured (some even dated on a fifty-two-week basis) that no time is left for elective units. Only the few who attend special discussion groups have the opportunity to grapple with serious questions about the church's responsibility in the world. One solution would be to publish undated units in teaching manuals. Another possibility is to write the concern directly into session plans either through the medium of story and discussion material or special projects or under the heading of "Ideas to Think About" in the teacher's introductory material.

Christianity has been encircling the globe ever since Paul and others began sailing the Mediterranean Sea to cities such as Pergamum. Today the Christian church has more adherents than does any other world faith. Currently its most intense growth is in the nations of Africa.

For more than a century Protestant Sunday church schools have had regular units of study about the world mission in individual countries. Returned missionaries on furlough brought congregations up-to-date on their work. Nationals visited churches and studied in colleges and seminaries. Today evangelical Christians have continued the tradition and their constituencies are aware of the challenges to the church today.

Orbis Books, operated by the Maryknoll Society, publishes significant books about issues facing the "younger" churches. Friendship Press publishes study materials on social concerns and outreach. As with areas of learning noted elsewhere, the omission of world mission concerns by many curriculum materials occurs because the concern is neither structured into regular materials and encouraged in introductory teacher materials, nor included as a possible unit within the course of study. Yet the knowledge about and encouragement of the proclamation of the Good News is a primary responsibility of all Christians.

Initiating the development of educational materials remains primarily with the planners at the publishing and editing level. The specific contribution at the local level will lie in the search for knowledgeable people who have been involved in this mission and can share their experiences. Returned travelers could be invited to share their impressions and show visual materials. Travelogues are helpful to the extent that knowledge about and appreciation of a culture introduces hearers to the broader questions of how the church is at work in that place.

The import of this chapter is to say that a study of the parish by people responsible for planning the educational program is essential if the best choices are to be made from among available curriculum material. Such a study will indicate the content, method, and theological viewpoint most compatible with the constituency. It will suggest the optimum age-level groups as well as possible areas of study for adolescents and adults. This information becomes available through surveys that indicate the education, work, interests, and community settings of church members.

About Goals and Evaluation

Early in any process of curriculum development it is essential to establish goals. To ascertain how goals are being met, it is equally important to set up procedures for evaluation. These two processes interact.

People speak about "purposes," "goals," and "objectives." The dictionary is not helpful in distinguishing among these terms because it uses the words interchangeably in definitions. In general, a purpose is something one hopes to accomplish. It is describable, but it is also visionary. It is the long-term goal.

Goals

The word "goal" is used concretely. Writers speak of "measurable goals," meaning goals specific enough to be subjected to evaluation procedures. People also speak of "behavioral goals," meaning that the goal is to be a change in the learners' behavior. The term "concrete objective" is also used interchangeably with "measurable goal." "Short-term" or "long-term" objectives are words meant to convey the time span of accomplishment.

Several sets of goals may interact. Teacher goals may not be the same as learner goals. This can result in a class's working at cross-purposes to a teacher with little visible accomplishment by either. A curricular planning group might be working without agreed-upon goals. Clergy may have one set of goals that they hope will be accomplished through the use of curriculum materials, teachers another, and parents a third.

With long-range goals, there need to be short-term objectives. In this situation, then, as a person moves from one group to another, progress will be made toward the long-range goal.

Some religious education programs have a goal vaguely described as "knowing the Bible." This goal needs to be clarified. What is meant by *knowing* the Bible? It could mean to memorize, understand, interpret, discover meaning, explore ways of interpretation, be able to apply the Bible to life, or appreciate the use of the Bible in worship and personal devotion. Some of the frustration behind the popularly held feeling in churches that "Little is learned in religious education classes" stems from the fact that no one ever described the learning goals.

Another dimension to goals comes from the publishers and editors' realm. Promotional materials usually list overall goals of curricula, although these are really selling points. Each course of study lists specific goals in the introductory materials. Teachers may not read these carefully enough, however, to "own" them for their own use.

A number of years ago, the United Presbyterian Church began the trend toward setting behavioral objectives by listing five areas of competency as the basis for its, curriculum.[1] It was their thesis that anyone who had studied that curriculum should be able to exhibit abilities developed in the areas of Bible, church, faith, Christian living, and ecumenical/worldwide attitudes.

The CE:SA materials have established goals for each of the four approaches. The goal of *Knowing the Word* is

> . . . to enable persons to know the contents of the Bible, to understand their experiences and relationships in the light of the Biblical message, and to recognize the tension between the truth of the Biblical message and persistent concerns of persons and society, to the end that they may respond as faithful disciples.[2]

Note that the key words are "to enable," a role that the teacher would play. The expected behavior on the part of learners is to "know contents . . . understand their experiences and . . . recognize the tension . . . [so] that they may respond. . . ." Content and methods of the curriculum are presumably designed to meet these goals.

The goal for *Interpreting the Word* is "to increase the ability of the people of God to respond to the Scriptures, equipping them to be responsible interpreters of Scripture." The manual then continues by explaining what is meant by "respond," and to be "responsible interpreters."[3]

The goal for *Living the Word* is "to enable persons to mature in faith as they participate in the life and mission of the Christian *community.*"[4] The manual continues by listing the special emphases of this approach, including the fact that material may begin either with biblical content or life situations. "It recognizes and utilizes the fact that all of the congregation's experiences teach."

These three sets of goals are presented as examples because they describe distinctive emphases within three approaches. By contrast, David C. Cook Publishing Co., an independent evangelical publisher, lists one overall purpose in its material, "to lead students to a personal faith in Christ and to live out their Bible learning in their life-relationships with others."[5]

Examination of the introductory pages of any curriculum should find a disclosure of the goals. Goals set forth in promotional material will be similar but probably simplified.

The National Council of Churches for many years has been involved in helping constituent bodies with curriculum planning.[6] In 1965 through the work of the Cooperative Curriculum Project it developed a new curriculum plan. Later their volume *Tools for Curriculum Development*, following the then popular approach of Bloom's *Taxonomies of Education*,[7] delineated competencies for each age level and in all areas on a graduated scale. In preference to "goal," it used the term "learning task" and enumerated five:

> Listening with growing alertness to the gospel and responding in faith and love. . . .
> Exploring the whole field of relationships in the light of the gospel.
> Discovering meaning and value in the field of relationships in light of the gospel.
> Appropriating personally the meaning and value discovered in the field of relationships in light of the gospel.
> Assuming personal and social responsibility in light of the gospel.[8]

Notice the behavioral words: listening, exploring, discovering, appropriating, assuming. The teacher's task would be to elicit and reinforce such behavior.

Such goals, established by the people who plan and produce curricular materials, are not drawn from thin air. They represent a balance between what the planners sense to be the goals of their constituency, with additions and modifications that reflect their own thinking as professionals about religious education. It is doubtful if people in parishes pay serious attention to the announced goals. Teachers feel that their main job is to read their teaching manual in order to make plans. They are less interested in long-range goals that explain the rationale of a curriculum. They are looking more for reassurance than for detailed analyses.

Some Roman Catholic publishers describe goals in terms of grade objectives. A Benziger, Bruce & Glencoe, Inc. book states that its material "emphasizes ideas that make a difference in the lives of children, and those traditions that give us an identity as the people of God in a program that provides a basis for shared spiritual growth."[9] The William H. Sadlier, Inc.'s program states, as an aim, "to establish a growing sense of community among families, catechists and priests; a deeper awareness of catechists and parents on the interdependence of their efforts in the education of the child. It is designed to provide opportunities for sharing and growing together in faith."[10] The Silver Burdett Co., in its prospectus, states that its program is designed to help teachers lay the foundation necessary for continued growth in faith. Winston Press, Inc. stresses sequential development across all areas of catechesis. Note here an emphasis on growing into the Christian community and on deepening faith. Notice also an emphasis on the interrelationships among parents, teachers, and clergy in fulfilling these goals.

When reading the goals of specific curricular materials, people need to learn how to distinguish between the promotional statements of an introductory leaflet and the goals announced within the curriculum itself. One such flyer announces its "True to the Bible" series, stating:

> By "true to the Bible" we mean, simply, that our writers and editors consider ALL that the Bible teaches about any given topic. Not just those Scriptures that agree with a particular doctrinal position. Every effort is made to present the Word of God without bias or preconceived ideas. Only in this way will your pupils get a true picture of the Bible. Only in this way will the Scriptures have real meaning for their lives.[11]

Clearly, this is advertising hyperbole. Any thoughtful person knows that everyone has a bias, a personal slant, and preconceived ideas. This is not meant to be a negatively critical statement but a description of how the human mind functions. Only by recognizing a bias can anyone compensate for it in order to be in any sense "objective." Phrases such as "true picture" and "real meaning" may be reassuring but they hardly give an accurate description of specific biblical interpretation. These materials, like all others, do in fact have a specific viewpoint toward biblical interpretation, and it is because of this viewpoint that some churches choose them over other available courses of study while others reject the materials as not consonant with their theological position.

This survey has presented a mixture of goals. Some are in the minds of denominational planners, growing out of their hopes for continually improving parish religious education programs. Some goals are held by independent publishers, somewhat determined by whether they need to sell their wares to a judicatory committee or a local church committee. There are also goals in the minds of local churches, teachers, parents, and clergy as they consider curricular options.

Goals in a Parish Perspective

It has been stated earlier that religious education is a subsystem within the total system that makes up a parish. There are five elements in the educational system: planning/evaluation, theological/educational assumptions, teaching/learning opportunities, material resources, and leader development and support.[12] No element in the system can function well unless all are in good order. Goal setting must precede any decision as to what approach to use or what combination of courses to select from among the possibilities.

Few churches have taken goal setting this seriously. If a teacher were asked, "Why did you substitute this material for that which was bought last fall?" the answer might be, "This one is easier to teach." The importance that teachers attach to format, session plans, simplicity of resources and ease of preparation must be taken into consideration in curriculum selection. Examination of a teacher's manual will indicate to what extent these criteria are being met.

Another goal that sets a criterion for choosing material, voiced by teachers and parents, is that learners shall "know the Bible." Because this goal is basic in Protestant thinking and important among Catholics, it is necessary to consider what the words really mean to those who hold the criterion. There is constant tension between curriculum planners and users over the ideas of knowing biblical content and interpreting the Bible, and applying the Bible to life and seeking biblical insights to interpret life experience. Some would apply the message of the Bible only to personal life; others hear the message addressed to societal problems. If parishes feel that "knowing the Bible" is basic to

Christian education, they need some impetus to probe more deeply into the meaning of the terms being used and to learn how these can be made concrete in methods of teaching as well as in materials for study.

Planners need also to describe what they mean by "living the Christian life," another widely held goal. Is it living by Christian principles and values or following Jesus or keeping the Bible's commandments? In what way does the Christian life indicate a personal response to God in Christ? Is there consensus as to what qualities of living exemplify or exhibit Christian faith? We are aware of being in the presence of a saintly person, but it is impossible to analyze the quality of saintliness, much less to imitate the example. One might define or describe Christian living by making a check-list of "dos" and "don'ts," but such a list would never reveal a quality of life. Christians, like other people, are mortal and sinful. What makes them different is not the degree of personal perfection so much as their awareness of participating in the fulfillment of God's purposes for all creation.

Or, consider Christian belief as a goal held by some people. The classical preparation for baptism in the late fourth century was a study of three basic documents: the creed, representing the faith of the church; the Ten Commandments, representing the rule of living; and the Lord's Prayer, representing the prayer of the church. Often these were used in catechetical lectures. In post-Reformation times the method of teaching was to use a series of questions and answers through which the learner demonstrated memorization of the materials. Today the emphasis is on understanding and being able to interpret basic beliefs. This is a concrete goal. By early adolescence, a person should grasp the basic meaning of the content, and the abilities to interpret meaning deeply and to ponder the relationship between the Commandments and their interpretation in the Sermon on the Mount should increase throughout life.

Christian belief is not primarily a matter of knowing, although the study of theology as an intellectual discipline has a distinguished history. Theology is a sophisticated development from credal statements. To state "I believe in God the Father almighty, maker of heaven and earth" is to express a trust in God and a relationship to God. The development of this relationship is one of the goals of any Christian education, but few will agree as to how it is to be accomplished, much less on how the fulfillment is to be evaluated.

Moreover, Christian faith sees God in Jesus Christ, and this uniquely Christian insight is more difficult to convey than most curriculum materials would suggest. It is easier to take an extreme liberal stance and talk about God the Creator and Jesus who by his words and deeds showed people how God acts. When even theologians debate if and how the concept of incarnation can have meaning for people today, one does not expect it to be a simple matter to incorporate this belief into religious education curriculum. The Christian affirmation of God as Trinity is equally difficult to convey. An understanding of the Holy Spirit and of the interrelationships that are named the Trinity are virtually absent from curriculum at any age level. In affirming the understanding of and growing relationship to God as a goal of Christian education, planners should be aware of how complicated a goal they are setting.

Many people involved in religious education would affirm the goal expressed earlier by a publisher as "leading students to a personal faith in Jesus Christ." The rituals for believer's baptism, confirmation, or church membership include an affirmation that the person accepts Jesus Christ as personal Lord and Savior. This is no simple statement. It involves theological understandings and personal commitment. Churches do not usually state what behavior they expect to exhibit commitment. Many congregations discover to their dismay that baptism or confirmation often seems to young people like a graduation from church.

In speaking of commitment to Christ one is also stating a goal about the church. Education has been a function of the Christian community since earliest times. This has been education for membership within the church as well as witness in all of life. Such education must include learning the meaning of the liturgy and how to participate in the liturgy, the history of the church, and its governmental structures. History is not simply the memorization of facts but participation in a life story that one learns to understand and appreciate. Every Christian group has evolved basic structures, and participation in these structures marks an individual's acceptance of the tradition.

Understanding of and participation in worship are basic. These include not only faithful attendance but also reflection upon what happens at the liturgy and the meaning of worship and learning the materials used for worship. These matters need to be structured into learning materials in such a way that the course helps learners to understand the worship service in which they are participants. At present Roman Catholic materials take this task seriously, especially in preparing children for their first Eucharist. Independent Protestant materials have virtually nothing on the subject and the denominationally sponsored materials usually are content to insert a course at some particular point. Church membership materials come too late in a child's experience to serve the need of the continuous incorporation of young learners into the worshiping community.

Commitment is expected to result in a life of service, of witness to the Good News in the immediate community and in all the world. Published goals diverge on how to interpret this service. Materials that call for "the examination of all of life in the light of the gospel" do not go very far in this examination. Denominational planners do not structure into materials specific ways of helping learners fulfill their baptismal promises. There is no postbaptismal/confirmation material through which to reflect on the experience. Independent Protestant publishers for the most part ignore this element. Even the traditional missions outreach is ignored. Curriculum planners, objecting to the insertion of special emphases, have found no way to acquaint learners with the remarkable way that the Christian message has spread around the globe or the exciting indigenous development of the church in many countries today.

Akin to this concern is the way in which the ecumenical dimension is ignored, even when announced as a goal.

What is the conclusion? When one considers the numbers of goals and the components of each goal, it becomes problematical how they can be fulfilled. Further, it is difficult to know how these can be stated as concrete or behavioral objectives. It is important to distinguish between goals for religious education and the more limited area of goals for the curriculum.

A serious study of goals by each congregation is a fundamental necessity before any curricular materials can be chosen. This should be done by a group that includes clergy, coordinators and/or superintendents, teachers, and parents. In relation to the adolescent and adult level, the study should also include learners. The goals are set on the basis of what is known of the makeup of the parish, the theological and biblical assumptions of its people and the denomination, and the potentialities for instruction in terms of building, equipment, resources, and potential teachers. The goals suggested here are only a beginning.

Evaluation

At the point of evaluation, anyone would long for concrete, measurable goals. How can one evaluate the development of "appreciation," or "understanding"? How does a teacher or parent know when children have been "helped to . . ."? Yet objectives are frequently stated in such terms. One reason for doing so may be to lessen the pressure to achieve—by either teachers or learners. Real achievement in Sunday church school or CCD class is made virtually impossible by the lack of training of teachers combined with the brief, even sporadic attendance by learners. But use of this argument could also become an evasion. If a religious education committee is committed to learning as a parish goal, then it must recognize the possibility that concrete change can take place through the process of education.

Correctly viewed, planning (goals) and evaluation are a continuous process. There can be no final "grade," because learners are growing people and many factors contribute to their experiences. Evaluation is a diagnostic tool that indicates which goals have been achieved and to what extent. Evaluation shows what has been learned, making it possible for planners to review the whole process. Was the goal achieved easily? Did it turn out to be an unrealistic expectation? Was it beyond the capabilities of the learners? Were the materials, resources, and/or methods adequate? Did the teacher and the learners fully understand the goal?

A decision might be reached that the goal was adequate but that changes in teaching methods were needed. One goal might not be capable of fulfillment until pupils were older, or it might require a longer time for completion. In the light of such findings, teachers and other leaders restructure the learning process for the next year.

It is important to understand that evaluation is not a judgment. No one should be looking for right or wrong, much less trying to determine who was right or wrong. The evaluation process seeks to discover how adequate were the goals themselves and what changes in the teaching process might facilitate their achievement. The next year, with a different group of learners and teachers, a goal which had earlier seemed excellent might turn out to be either too difficult or too easy. Goals are not "ideals" in any abstract sense. They are planned for the use of real teachers and learners living within a complex environment of family, church, and community. The specific Sunday or weekday setting for a class is only one factor in learning.

Such a view of the planning/evaluation process is dynamic because it offers opportunity for continuous change. The process can be flexible when people remain aware of the variables in the teaching situation. Everyone involved in the situation may participate. Evaluation should always be viewed as a tool in the learning process, along with goal setting and other elements. It is not an end product. The distinction is important when trying to persuade people in churches to evaluate a program. These are nonprofessionals who volunteer their time out of devotion to the cause of Christian education. They do not wish to be evaluated in what they would view as a professional way. When they understand that the evaluation is not being made of the *teacher* but of the *process* and that they play an important part in helping to reassess the process, they will be able to view evaluation in a nonthreatening perspective.

Turn again to the goals and consider how each might be evaluated constructively. Begin with the goal concerned with knowledge of the Bible. The goal should include the essential material that all learners are expected to remember, for example, at the end of grade six (during a period of concrete learning) and further learning to be accomplished between grades nine through twelve. Material to be learned should grow more complex with each retelling; otherwise it will be merely repetitive to the learner and become boring.

The next aspect of biblical study is understanding. This has two facets: interpretation of what the writer probably meant, and some insight as to what this can mean for lives today. Interpretation is a skill that learners develop at about eleven years of age when they are beginning to think abstractly. Learners need to develop skills in using resource materials, such as a concordance, commentary, atlas, wordbook, and biblical dictionary. Young people are accustomed to this kind of study in school.

Understanding the meaning of the Bible for life can begin with a selection of verses that assure the child of God's love and care. Probing the meaning of a passage becomes more critical when learners are asked to look at their actions in family and community in the light of the biblical word and may even become controversial. Many would rather leave the prophets' demands for justice in a biblical setting than to ask whether there are similarities in our own society.

These are three aspects of biblical study that need to be evaluated. Knowledge can be assessed because information can be repeated in oral or written form. Quizzes give an opportunity to choose the correct answer by multiple choice, fill-ins, or arranging people or events in chronological order. The time-line, written from memory at the conclusion of historical study, is another way of testing retained knowledge. Remember that the test is designed, not to frighten the pupil and judge the teacher, but to indicate if the expectations of the pupil with this material were too high or too low, if the material was too easy or too difficult, and if the methods and resources available were adequate for the kind and amount of learning that was expected to occur. These questions will give some indication about the adequacy of a particular course of study for meeting specific goals.

Biblical interpretation can also be ascertained informally through multiple choice. For example: "Look up Amos 5:24, and underline one of three sentences that comes nearest to what he meant by his statement." Or a sentence or passage can be assigned for study and the result shared either orally or by written answers, using resource books to test the students' ability to use such aids.

"What does the Bible say to me?" is a more difficult area to evaluate because there is no *one* correct answer. An answer might be couched in general terms ("This passage teaches me to be honest") while the specific nature of the application is left unclear. Moreover, correct thinking is not synonymous with action when a real situation arises. The situational passage and its answer give a helpful way of *envisioning* response to biblical teaching, but this still remains in the realm of theory. The way in which learners act in the class situation is a limited but more realistic estimate of moral and ethical understandings of human relationships, if the actions seem clearly to be in response to the Bible and not to conformity with parental rules or societal expectations. Through outreach projects learners can develop ways of witnessing to their faith.

There is one more dimension. The Christian life is a response to the grace of God, lived in joyful thanksgiving. People who try hard to keep the biblical law and are anxious when they or others fail have not fully understood the freedom to be found in such response. It is difficult to know how to encourage such people to live more freely. However, when a person shares ways in which the Bible has been a strengthening influence and has given direction to life, a response is being made. Probably a number of factors were involved, including personal devotion, regular Bible study, meditation, faithful attendance at worship, and continuous practice of Christian obedience.

There are limits both to how far a curriculum can be expected to carry a goal and to what extent every goal of Christian education can be evaluated. These limitations should not prevent religious education leaders from trying. Goal setting offers a way through which educational efforts can be improved.

The process outlined here could be extended to a study of other goals, ways of working toward their completion, and evaluation of the extent to which they have been met. One can learn about God, be taught how to pray, and understand what it means to be a member of the Christian community, but the total dimension of the relationship of the believer to God is beyond measurement by the tools for evaluation. Persons can be nurtured and taught steps toward the goal of commitment to Christ, and some materials are designed to accomplish conversion. Some church traditions prefer that the commitment come through involvement in the life of the worshiping community. Most prepare young people for church membership at a particular age. Methods and materials cannot guarantee that the commitment is made for life nor reveal what the profession of faith really means to the individual. The goal of such teaching can be only that of preparation for the event.

Evaluation has its limitations and its usefulness. Reality consists in knowing in advance which goals can be tested and which cannot and in keeping a balance. This is a continuing work for thoughtful planners, teachers, and learners. The reward is in knowing with some certainty how the educational process is functioning.

Chapter

Considering Biblical and Theological Assumptions

Choosing curriculum options includes having a clear idea of what a church believes. Producers of curriculum have theological, biblical, and educational assumptions in mind in designing objectives, developing material, and working with editors and writers. A curriculum can appeal to people across a fairly wide spectrum of beliefs, but there are limits. Some curricula are deliberately designed to meet the theological needs of a particular denomination.

Assumptions About the Bible

Assumptions about the Bible are central to any religious education curriculum. Curriculum contains definitions of truth and fact and the relationship between them. Some curricula affirm that every statement in the Bible is both fact and truth. Others affirm that biblical statements are true but not necessarily factual. The former is referred to as the doctrine of biblical inerrancy. This doctrine reflects the belief that the biblical material must be factual because the God who inspired it cannot err. To say that God can err presents a contradiction for anyone who affirms that God is all knowing. A related doctrine is that of biblical inspiration. Some affirm that because the Bible is inspired by the Holy Spirit, the books in it cannot include factual errors. Others say that God inspired the writers, but that they wrote as human beings, reflecting their own times. Some affirm that to speak of the Scripture as the Word of God is to affirm the facticity of every word of Scripture. Others affirm that Scripture is the Word because it witnesses to God's Word and, ultimately, to the Word made flesh in Jesus Christ.

Some say that the authority of the Bible lies in its being the very word of God and that every word in the Scriptures is to be believed and obeyed. Others say that the authority of the Bible lies in the fact that it describes how God acts and thereby shows who God is. It is authoritative in what is said about God, but it is also limited by the people who wrote it and by their sometimes imperfect understanding of God's word and will. Some take the revealed Word of God to mean that every statement in the Bible has been revealed as divine word and action. Others understand revelation to mean the self-disclosure of God to humans, Scripture being the vehicle for the revelation. While there may be other ways that God is revealed (some see this happening through the natural world or through human love and concern), the Scriptures are the primary mode of God's self-disclosure.

In summary, here are some basic theological words that have reference to interpreting the Bible. They are important in the selection of curriculum: truth, fact, inerrancy, inspiration, authority, and revelation. These words may not be found in the actual teaching materials, but they may appear in the teacher's introductory material and may also be found in whatever promotional or explanatory material the publisher makes available.

For example, the David C. Cook Publishing Co. prints the five fundamentals of evangelical belief in material written for prospective buyers.[1] The CE:SA material says: "The Bible is uniquely authoritative for Christians. . . . The Holy Spirit who inspired the writers of the Bible also illumines the hearts and minds of its readers and interpreters."[2]

The Bible, for most Christians, can be interpreted as the covenant between God and God's people—as the Christian designation of its two sections connotes, Old Testament and New Testament. It is a book of promise, a note that should be made clear in any curriculum that seeks faithfully to interpret Scripture. This does not mean that the word of judgment, found throughout the Bible, can be ignored but only that the promise of salvation and the word of judgment must be viewed together as facets of God's action. The Bible is also a book of historic records, telling about real people in their times and geographic settings. It is not a book of philosophy, speculating on the existence and attributes of God. It does not relate myths of prehistory as do, for example, the Hindu scriptures in the *Ramavana*. Some biblical books record the human search for God, a note that can be heard in the cries of the psalmists and of Job and his friends.

Some teaching materials lay more stress on the wonder stories of the Bible: healings and miraculous events. Some emphasize its teaching: the commands in both Old and New Testaments and stories that illustrate how people fulfilled or disobeyed those commands. Some materials indicate the continuity between Old and New Testaments. Others emphasize the use of New Testament materials—primarily the Gospels.

Another approach to understanding the Bible is through a study of its composition.[3] The canon, the collection of sixty-six books (and, for some, the Apocrypha), is basic. These books were collected and affirmed as the Scriptures for the Christian church at an early point in its history. This fact does not preclude inquiry as to how the books developed. As everyone knows, the Dead Sea Scrolls, since their discovery in 1948, have been an important asset in uncovering the earliest canon for the Hebrew Scriptures and in comparing the accuracy of both translations and copying. The Isaiah scroll dates from the first century—hundreds of years earlier than any manuscript known up to that time. Textual criticism is one of the ways through which scholars try to uncover the earliest form of the biblical word.

Another kind of critical study is literary criticism, an inquiry into the forms of literature represented by the writings. The books of First and Second Samuel, First and Second Kings, and First and Second Chronicles as well as Ezra-Nehemiah are historical records. They document the rise of the United Kingdom, its fall, the reigns of the kings of Israel and Judah, and the return from exile. The book of Psalms includes many kinds of songs liturgical and personal: songs of praise, petition, and lamentation. The books of the prophets include not only their own oracles—proclamation of God's word—but biographical, autobiographical and historical materials. The Gospels are a unique literary form, while the book of the Acts is a historical chronicle, some of it written evidently by an eyewitness. Letters, like those of Paul, are forms found frequently in literature.

Form criticism is another approach to understanding how the Bible was written. Form critics were the first scholars to look carefully at the book of Psalms to see the different types of prayers and anthems that it contains. They have looked at other collections of wise sayings to help understand the book of Proverbs. Scholars have compared the Gospels to find reasons for both repetitions and omissions in them. Some sayings will have a different setting in each of two Gospels; one event such as the giving of the Lord's Prayer, may be found in two different settings. Why, scholars ask, are the birth stories given in only two Gospels, each relating a different aspect of the narrative? Why are the resurrection narratives scattered among all four Gospels? What was the purpose of the narratives, and what were the interpretations? There are parables, pronouncement stories, wonder stories, and other forms. The answers to such questions help readers of the Bible to understand Jesus as both a person of his time and as one who was viewed as unique by his followers.

Redaction criticism has been a recent approach based on the affirmation of the canon as the received text. By examining the work of the final editors (redactors) scholars try to gain new insights into how a book was put together. Many biblical books, including the Gospels, began as oral traditions—sayings and stories handed down by individuals and Christian communities. Not until a generation after the beginnings of the church were these written down. This means that letters of Paul predate the Gospels as written documents.

The most recent approach to biblical study is Structuralism. In a highly complicated manner scholars seek to analyze the structure of a particular story (such as the story of Joseph or one of the parables) to try to uncover from its structure something about how and why the story developed.

Some understanding of the breadth of biblical studies should be important to those whose task it is to choose curriculum materials. Producers of curriculum, editors, and writers must take the composition of the Bible seriously even if there will be no direct reference to the matter. Whether or not writers are aware of critical study, however, will quickly become apparent to anyone reading the material. This is indicated by the kind of introduction to a biblical passage given in the adult material and the way in which high school students or adults are introduced to biblical background materials. Young people and adults know about the existence of critical studies in other fields. Sometimes in the church they are not encouraged to make inquiries about the Bible.

Foundations for biblical study begin with materials for children. They need to see biblical people as real persons rather than idealized versions that either omit their wrongdoings or use these only to point morals for young readers. The marvelous work of creation is conveyed in the sense of wonder the teacher gives to the phrase "In the beginning God. . . ." This sense of mystery and wonder is not enhanced by an approach that attempts to prove a six-day creation. The Book of Isaiah becomes more impressive to those who realize that its message was written during a time span that included the exile. Teachers should not give the impression that the person who spoke to King Uzziah was the same person whose assurances of restoration are to be found in the later chapters. Materials should convey respected scholarly understanding of how the Bible was written. People who choose curriculum need to inquire into their own understandings and to be sufficiently conversant with biblical study in order to recognize the interpretations used by editors and writers.

Another aspect of the use of the Bible in curriculum lies in how story material is presented. One aspect has already been mentioned: the need to see a person's life in its entirety. This precludes attempts to make a hero out of Jacob or of young Joseph. Each belonged to the family with whom the covenant had been made. Each was in some way fulfilling the covenant through his life, but neither was perfect. Peter is another person whose life is not always presented in its wholeness: a disciple who was both loyal and vacillating. Yet these very ambiguities make Peter human like all other Christians. Those who hear and read the Gospel story can see themselves in the people who came to Jesus for help: some in faith and some unbelieving; some accepting his offer to follow him and others turning aside. Are we not among both those who cried out, "Hosanna!" and those who later cried, "Crucify him!"? Teaching materials need to help learners identify with those who came to Jesus, both in their weaknesses and in their strengths.

More nonstory materials could be used. Verses of thanksgiving and reassurance from the Psalms would be more helpful to small children than many of the Bible stories that parents desire and teachers tell. Children in the Bible stories are frequently in distress: Ishmael, Isaac, Joseph, Moses, Samuel—even though each story has a happy ending. Some stories about adults might be more parallel to the experience of a child needing help and forgiveness. Among older children and adults material from the prophets can be used effectively because this deals profoundly with social justice. The Psalms speak to many human situations.

Some passages could be used for summarizing and reflecting on the history of the covenant, for example, Psalm 136.

Although the Bible is used in worship, curricular material seldom refers to the connection between the Scriptures used in worship and the Scriptures used in teaching. Critics of the Sunday church school affirm that attendance at the liturgy is a better way to learn the meaning of the Bible than is the "schooling" situation.[4] In traditions that use a lectionary, the Sunday readings are known in advance and could be incorporated into the structure of a curriculum. Another way would be to use a lectionary-based curriculum, but this has the same disadvantages as the Uniform Lesson Series outlines in that not all material is readily adaptable for use with young children. In preparation for their own participation in worship, children need to be helped to interpret the Lord's Prayer. They could be shown the continuity in the use of the Psalms from biblical times to the present. They can look up in the Bible the call to worship, offertory sentences, and benediction when these are from the Bible. This is a point at which both independent and cooperative curricula are weak, and only through parish planning can this important learning be inserted into the curriculum.

Theology in the Curriculum

Curriculum materials indicate some presuppositions about the understanding of God. This is not always made explicit in introductory material. The Bible gives concrete expression of the activity of God. It does not speculate on the existence of God. Today many people are seekers, and the search for belief usually includes speculative questions. Few curricular materials ever take this approach. This means that they do not speak to some of the needs of prospective learners. In teaching it is important to begin with their questions before giving biblical and traditional faith answers.

Materials for children that look at the world as revelatory of God's presence raise questions about the goodness of God. If the world is supposed to reveal God's care, why are there natural disasters such as earthquakes, tornadoes, and hurricanes that destroy helpless people? The workings of the providence and mercy of God are mysteries not open to human understanding. Teachers will want to be careful that children are not given easy answers through the materials presented.

The doctrine of salvation or redemption is at the heart of

Christian theology. It is a way of describing how God acted in Jesus Christ as Good News that all people may be saved from sin, suffering, and death, and given eternal life. Across the centuries theologians have described this in at least three ways, each stemming from biblical materials. The oldest, chronologically, is the "ransom" theory, based on Mark 10:45, "The Son of man came . . . to give his life as a ransom for many." It reflects a situation in the early centuries when many people had become enslaved through wars and the paying of a ransom would buy their release. So, said the theologian Irenaeus, Jesus by his life, death, and resurrection has ransomed us from the power of Satan and we are free not to sin but to live the new life in him.

The substitutionary theory is attributed to Anselm of Canterbury (eighth century) and came out of the juridical system, seeing human beings in the presence of God for judgment. Because God is just, all humans are guilty of breaking God's law. They deserve eternal punishment, but God loves people and wills their restoration. Jesus, voluntarily giving up his sinless life to the power of evil, became the substitute, and people are freed.

The moral influence theory of Abelard, several centuries later, came out of a rejection of the idea that God could condemn his own son, "rewarding" goodness and obedience this way. Rather, Abelard said, the crucifixion and resurrection show Christians how to live sacrificially and selflessly so that they, too, will be raised into eternal life.

The church has never declared any one of these interpretations of the death and resurrection of Jesus to be the only acceptable one. But, in fact, materials that dwell on theological interpretations tend to use the substitutionary theory. "Christ died for your sins" usually reflects this understanding. Learners whose thinking goes beyond the repetition of the phrase may wonder why God would design this way of saving the world. Or they may reject the idea of someone being sacrificed on their behalf. It is questionable what such an abstract statement can mean to five-year-old children or how to interpret it to older children. Adolescents and adults should be able to think abstractly and to wrestle with doctrine. Material should reflect the understandings of the people who are using it.

The most puzzling Christian doctrine for adherents of other religions is that of the Trinity. Christians do not worship three gods but one God whom they understand as three "persons."

The word "person" reflects its original Greek usage referring to the masks an actor would wear. God is known in three ways, three aspects. The term is descriptive, not definitive—an important distinction. Looked at in terms of curriculum, one would ask how the "mystery," the wonder of this understanding of God, can have meaning. When children are taught to use the terms God and Jesus interchangeably in prayer, they may regard this as using two names for God or as addressing two different persons. Adolescents may understand alternatively Jesus of Nazareth and an abstract Christ-Spirit. Notice how frequently liturgical prayer is addressed to God in the name of Jesus Christ and the Holy Spirit. This represents a longtime effort of the church to keep in perspective the unity of God. It might be well to do this consistently in teaching materials.

Other questions about theological understanding are raised under the discussion of goals. The final question to ask is who sets agreed-upon theological interpretations for the curriculum—the teacher (who wants materials that are theologically agreeable), the religious education committee, parents (who have convictions that they think should be in the material), or the minister (who is theologically educated)? If such questions are not answered and, particularly, if curriculum materials are ordered from various publishers without referring to the theological factor, there may be in use materials that work at cross-purposes and bring confusion to learners. This may be one reason why many Christians, unless they are from a Roman Catholic or an evangelical background, do not often know how to explain their beliefs.

Being a Christian

Because people study as members of the Christian community, curriculum materials need to convey understandings about the nature and meaning of the church. Small children are taken to see different parts of the building and its furnishings; older children study the symbolism. Occasionally deeper questions stemming from New Testament origins will appear in adult material. The meaning of the church, the significance of the divine and human elements, the relationship of origins to later manifestations, the meaning of "fellowship"—all have different interpretations among Christian groups. Among the Reformation traditions there arose distinctions that persist today. Curriculum materials reflect meanings.

Witness and evangelism are other terms to be clarified. Some people virtually ignore the words; others make them the basis for membership recruitment. Neither reflects the biblical meaning. At a time when products are being sold with fervor through television and other media, Christians need to be clear on the distinction they make between "selling" and "proclaiming" the Good News. Knowing the meaning of words is an educational task, and curriculum materials should be vehicles for such learning.

It used to be said that one goal was to teach people how to live as Christians, or, as we would say more recently, develop a Christian life-style. This raises more questions about terminology. There is a difference between "morality" and "moralism." The former refers to a way of living, but the latter is construed to refer to the keeping of rules. A person could be anxious about keeping the rules and miss the basic response to God's grace that is the mark of a Christian life. If there is a distinction between Christian morality and being a moral person, it would have to be in the intention: the Christian life is a reflection of God's love and a response to grace. Some curriculum materials seem to equate Christian living with obedience to parents or with not making intentionally false statements, even out of loyalty. Yet the materials never deal with the deeper aspects of Christianity that make obedience a response in love or probe the ambiguity between honesty and loyalty. Another matter to be considered is the relationship of law to grace. Without ignoring law, grace recognizes human frailty. All these words in the Christian vocabulary need to be taught in order to be understood.

There is also the matter of relationships: what does it mean to live as a Christian among family and friends, in school and community, as citizens of nations and the world? Christian groups differ in their understandings. Some permit divorce and remarriage; others do not. Some recognize a just war; others do not. Some stress personal morality: if everyone lived as a Christian there would be no social problems. Others believe that social justice must be accomplished by law. Decision making in family relationships, business situations and community life causes anguish among many people today.

These raise the question of what it means to be a Christian "in the world." Israel affirms itself to be a Jewish state with the Bible as the source for its law-making. Islamic states are developing a national life based on the Koran. Without being legally declared a "Christian" state, what would be the characteristics of a nation whose population is predominantly Christian? Curricular materials might well explore the subject. The materials chosen by any congregation should reflect its people's interpretation of Christian living.

These are some of the questions involved in exploring the theological bases for a curriculum.

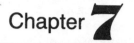

Chapter 7

Looking at Educational Assumptions

Teachers, clergy, and others involved in teaching are concerned about the content of curriculum. They want to know that the material reflects the beliefs of their tradition and its understanding of the Bible. People are more likely to sense ideas with which they disagree than to be aware of the underlying theological perspective of a curriculum.

This is equally true when analyzing educational assumptions. Teachers will frequently characterize materials as either teachable or not teachable. The former are, in their minds, clearly outlined and easy to follow, utilizing activities and resources that are readily available to most churches. The latter seem complicated or require too much initiative on the part of the teacher. These, however, are generalizations, no matter how relevant to the teacher's experience. Educational assumptions are more subtle and less easily analyzed.

To begin with, both goals and theological assumptions affect methods. If one goal is to "know" the Bible in the literal sense of memorizing passages such as the Ten Commandments, the Beatitudes, Psalms, and other significant materials, then methods for memorizing will be needed. These will include the use of the chalkboard for visualization, memory cards, games that encourage recall of contents, and wall charts so that the material can be seen whenever pupils are in the room.

When interpretation is a goal, there will be an emphasis on tools for research, interpretative passages in the teacher's manual to be shared with the class, and discussion questions, such as "If you were living in Israel in Amos' day, how do you think you would have responded to . . .?" or "What do you think this passage says for us today?"

When communication to others is the goal, methods will encourage the learner to retell the story in written or visual form. When the goal is applying the Bible to life experiences, the methods will involve role playing, open-ended stories, and discussions about the relationship of the Bible to life. They will also include projects of social concern.

The Nature of Learning

To examine the educational assumptions of a curriculum, one needs to understand something about the process of learning. People can learn through all of their experiences. They may also ignore experience and repeat events, including mistakes, without learning from them. Only by reflecting on experiences do people learn. Then they can decide whether the experience is worth repeating, should be modified, or should be ignored.

Repetition and reinforcement are essential elements in learning. Repetition can become so routine that a person repeats actions or words thoughtlessly. An optimum amount of repetition, however, leads to memorization of words or actions, an increase in skills, and the feeling of assurance that comes from competence. Reinforcement is the process by which correct learning is encouraged. When a child answers correctly, the teacher's "well done" encourages remembering. When a skill is perfected, satisfaction enhances the possibility of continuance. When work is rewarded, people are encouraged to continue because of the approval.

This suggests that teaching materials need to be structured to meet the learning abilities of any given age, remembering that there will be a variety of potentials within a class. The most successful materials will be those with a core of basic learning that includes suggestions for those who want to do more work or inquire more deeply. Dissatisfaction occurs in classrooms where learners either do not understand the materials or are quickly finished and become bored.

Materials also should arouse the curiosity of learners, by including what is already known while encouraging broad and deeper exploration. Learners need activities that utilize their skills and that can be completed competently.

Learning is an activity. Listening, by itself, is sometimes too passive to eventuate in learning. The recall of material heard is low unless the learner is highly motivated. The learner needs to be told in advance what kind of response will be expected: to retell the material, to answer questions about meaning, or to apply the information to a situation. The ineffectiveness of much adult material arises because teachers ignore this fact. Adult classes are expected to listen to material read or retold from a text but seldom are asked to respond in any serious way.

Learning occurs when the needs of the learners are being met. Sometimes attending a class is done primarily for the purpose of mutual support. The learning, then, comes from an informal and intangible response of people to one another. Children frequently attend religious education classes simply because their parents expect them to do so. The burden is then on the teacher (and the material) to discover the child's needs and interests.

Instruction is not the same as learning. Instruction is the teacher's function; learning is the pupil's activity. Instruction is an essential part of the learning process, particularly in intentional settings such as a religious education class. The development of teaching skills is essential, and the help offered by the material for this purpose is important. Leader development is a key to assisting teachers to utilize fully their material. Curricular materials are addressed to the instructor, but they presumably reflect a knowledge about learners and of how people learn. Those who choose curriculum materials must keep both facets in mind.

Teaching and learning are two elements in an interacting process. Understanding the learning process plus using methods and materials skillfully help the teacher to communicate with the learner. Then the pupil will be able to reflect on the experience in such a way as to be able to communicate the outcomes not only to the teacher but also to others.

The Learner

The learner is the one for whom materials are ultimately designed, although the teacher is the one most likely to make the choice of materials to be used. One criterion for choosing curriculum is whether the materials are suited to the learning capabilities of a particular age level. If materials are too difficult, the class becomes discouraged; if they are too simple, pupils are bored. Children who are bored find ways of expressing hostility; adolescents simply stay home.

Materials written today frequently are designed to meet the learning categories popularized from the writings of the Swiss psychologist, Jean Piaget.[1] His theory states that the development of learning parallels the development of particular capacities within the brain structure. Learning takes place through joint processes of assimilation, by which the learner takes into the organism new learning, and accommodation, by which the learning structures of the organism adapt to the new learning. The infant learns through sensorimotor activity, searching and finding in order to learn about the environment. The preschool child learns through "pre-operational" behavior; that is, through play activities and other direct experiences.

In early childhood (ages seven to eleven) learning takes place through "concrete operational" thinking. This is the time when schools emphasize developing concrete skills with words and numbers and when children learn how to read. Those considering religious educational materials should note the extent to which materials utilize such skills, giving children the opportunity to read for themselves and to reflect on their reading. Later in the concrete operational stage, they should also be able to respond to or retell what has been learned through writing or oral forms.

By junior-high age, children begin to develop the capacity to think abstractly and to conceptualize. Now they can begin biblical interpretation and understand the description of the Christian faith to be found in the historic confessions of faith.

Learners feel as well as think, and emotional components can either encourage or block cognitive learning. The psychosocial developmental categories of Erik Erikson are essential information for curriculum planners.[2] Writers of preschool curriculum should take into account the need that nurturing fulfills when a nursery is planned for children under two years. The development of autonomy (freedom and boundaries) is important for three-year-olds, and the encouragement of initiative (being oneself) should be evident in materials for the four-to five-year-olds. In the latter age group, children are also developing role and gender identity and a sense of conscience which, for them, is the internalized rules of the parent. This necessitates paying attention to both story and picture illustrations of the roles people play and being sensitive as to how children understand what it means to keep the rules. Piaget also speaks to this point.[3] The school-age child gains confidence through the successful development and use of skills, again pointing to the importance of serious learning experiences for this age. Adolescents are seeking self-identity, a quest that should be addressed in materials designed for their use.

This is not to suggest that religious education materials should repeat what the daily school is trying to do but that a knowledge of how persons develop can enhance the use of biblical and theological material in a curriculum.

Curricular resources for adults rarely indicate any awareness that chronologically mature people also are in stages of development. There is too little awareness in the way biblical materials are applied to life and in the selection of optional curricular units to deal with their various concerns. The interests of young adults revolve around the establishment of their lives with other persons and in careers. Middle-aged adults are concerned with intergenerational relationships and with their place in career and community, including church; older adults are engaged in a process of simplification of life and need to be able to view their lives as significant and to view their death as a positive ending.

The emotions evoked by material constitute another factor in learning. A story that arouses anxiety or hostility because of memories it evokes or fears it arouses will be resisted. Some biblical material may be frightening to children, depending partly on how it is presented. The story of the offering of Isaac is not really children's material, no matter how happy the outcome. It would be a strange way to teach children that God is faithful to the promise. Other stories carry a similar message. The children of the Bible seem almost invariably to be in precarious circumstances or separated from their families, one of the most frightening of imagined or real experiences for young children. Those who use biblical stories have a responsibility to examine the context in which the story is retold and the manner in which it is written.

Biblical material will be rejected by the learner if it seems to present idealized people. Older children as well as adolescents know how real people act in the real world. Attempts to present biblical persons like Abraham, Moses, David, and Paul without blemish will only invite rejection, especially if these characters are presented as models for young people. Moreover, if young people should persist in church life until they are old enough to hear or read the whole story, they may reject their religious education as dishonest.[4]

The Teaching Process

The interaction of learner and teacher takes place through the methods employed. The term "methods" refers to the techniques used in teaching. Back of all methods is the methodology, the underlying theory by which particular methods are chosen.

If learning is based on experiencing, techniques will include those through which learners can participate directly. Preschool rooms are set up with learning centers that assist young children to approximate their lives in families and with peers. There will be a housekeeping center, building blocks, trucks, and large toys for motor activity, a reading corner, and a listening corner. Specific forms of teaching will be carried on in those settings. The kindergarten curriculum for the Southern Baptist Sunday School Board is an excellent example. The learning center is the only kind of setting offered the teacher. The story material, half biblical and half experience-oriented, is designed to be told by teachers and helpers to small groups of children in a listening or reading center or in the "family" setting of the housekeeping corner. A simple prayer of thanksgiving is an act of worship in these settings.

Some people insist that children should be gathered into a circle to listen to the Bible story, learn songs, and pray together before engaging in activity work. This can make an inviting session under the guidance of skilled teachers with children able or accustomed to enjoy quiet modes of learning but neglects the possibilities for communication available in the informal setting.

A different methodology is the foundation for the use of learning centers with children in grades one through six. This approach is based on implications from Piaget's thought. It provides learners with opportunities to choose activities with which they are most comfortable in order to learn at their individual levels of achievement. The approach guards against random sampling of activities by outlining specific goals both for the course and for the learning contacts of each pupil.[5]

An "essentialist" or "classical learning" approach concentrates on a formal structure with content learning as a goal. Learners read the story and relevant biblical material, discuss the meaning, and express their understanding of the material orally or in writing. They would use reference works to discover meanings and share their findings with the class. The same teaching elements are present as in the learning center approach but are not offered at the same time. The "flow" of the session is more structured. Beginnings, transitions, and endings follow a pattern from one method to the next, such as presentation, exploration, affirmation, and application, or some other schema.

Methodology for curricular materials with adolescents frequently is based on a schema of presenting a life situation, seeking a biblical parallel, and raising questions for discussion. Materials for evening youth groups are usually more imaginative in design and more open in approach than are those used for formal teaching situations. Curriculum planners who understand the needs of youth in a parish may wish to examine a variety of material available for Sunday morning, evening groups, camps, conferences, and retreats and feel free to use any of these in any situation. The more traditional approach may be the least likely to attract adolescents to classes.

Methodology for adult materials has been even more restricted. Editors whose materials are based on the Uniform Lessons Series may even instruct writers that adults gathered in these classes expect a presentation by the leader with some questions for discussion. Perhaps some hope for innovative written materials for adult classes will come from Roman Catholic sources. The whole idea of parish adult education is still so new in Catholic circles that leaders in adult religious education are not hampered by stereotypical patterns from the past. They are open to group-oriented techniques, the use of film and tape, and varied resources.[6] The rationale for adult religious education has not been explicated for a long time in Protestant circles. While several denominations offer a wide diversity of content area options, even then the methods have tended to be "traditional" rather than innovative, despite a wise diversity in theme, ranging from social justice to personal devotions.

Although the teaching process is dependent on discovering the methodology that best fits the goals and capability of the learners and on methods or techniques, there are other elements. Learning depends on identifications. A primary identification is with the teacher whose attitude can encourage or discourage learning, invoke or block response, be open or opposed to inquiry. The teacher's manner of expressing personal convictions may invite or repel acceptance. The knowledgeable teacher feels free to act spontaneously and to make learning lively. The teacher who knows only the bare essentials in the book may seem to give a dull presentation. Teachers who can cope with experience-oriented situations, either in the classroom or in teaching materials, convey assurance. The use of a variety of methods can help to make a session interesting. Editors and writers try to include in the teacher's introductory material information and suggestions that will impart confidence to untrained teachers as new ways of teaching and of inviting free responses from the class are tried.

Some of the most basic teaching techniques require no special equipment and can be used by all teachers skilled in eliciting response from learners. Good teaching first invites the learner to observe what a biblical passage is saying or what is happening in a situation. Then the learner is invited to inquire about what the meaning is. Learning involves exploration and discovery. The combination of observation, inquiry, and discovery is basic to the education that children and youth receive in schools and that many adults use in daily work. In order for learners to feel comfortable with the methods outlined in a curriculum, the curriculum must utilize the tools of learning to which people are accustomed. Those who plan congregational curriculum need to be aware of the degree of correspondence between the learning techniques used in materials and the techniques already known by learners.

Another factor is the use of questions and answers in curriculum. Some courses of study employ only questions that expect essentially a repetition of information previously given. This kind of question is useful when a teacher wants to review before continuing with new material or to inform pupils who have been absent. Such recall can be provided in a more interesting way through games or quizzes.

Questions for discussion invite the learner to probe the thought of a writer. Other questions stimulate learners to reflect on events in the world, community, family, or church. This kind of probing has gained a certain popularity under the label of "action-reflection" method. As the Brazilian educator Paulo Freire has pointed out, action and reflection are inseparable components of the learning process.[7] This combination could make a dynamic curriculum either through direct experience or through vicarious action as reflected in a film, drama, novel, short story, or television program.

While forms of discussion, story telling, and certain other

activities require only a teacher's skill, other methods that would enhance learning require equipment. These methods may be so useful that churches should seriously consider gradually building up resources instead of rejecting particular methods as useless or too complicated for their situation. In the process of teaching/learning, whatever contributes to fulfilling the goal should be considered.

Creative and constructive methods so popular in curriculum materials for children need to be assessed. Frequently these are provided for in a workbook, which, with its variety of approaches, can be a delight to young learners but may seem repetitive if the workbook is a staple in daily school experience. Workbooks have the advantage of providing untrained teachers with ways of keeping children interested—unless the exercises are too simple, leaving some learners with time for boredom. Weigh both the advantages and disadvantages of spending money for workbooks. When a workbook is an integral part of the curriculum, a decision for or against its use is a decision concerning the whole course of study.

Some curricula do not use workbooks but offer teachers freedom to develop activities, such as posters, murals, or drawings to illustrate stories; hymns; biblical verses; time-lines; and maps. Children are familiar with these methods from school experience. In the thinking of teachers, activities are an important aspect of curriculum materials. Choose carefully. If there are so many suggestions that choice seems difficult, teachers will reject the material. If there are too few choices and these do not seem to fit the situation ("show the filmstrip" or "plan a party for . . ."), they will reject the material. If there are not clear directions for carrying out an activity or there is no encouragement for trying a new activity, teachers will reject the material. Religious educators must look carefully at the methods suggested and the way that these are introduced.

The use of methods in written curriculum is one of the critical areas where there has been divergence in practice between the publishers/editors and the parish teachers. The former understand clearly that the methods used reflect the interpretation of goals. For this reason, they have encouraged the use of what they call "creative" methods, by which is meant methods in which the learner is encouraged to express learnings through the use of various media and in accordance with individual interpretation. After a story has been told, it might be dramatized. This is not easy to do because children need careful direction in order to sort out the situation and roles and feel themselves into both. A less "creative" approach would be to use stick figures from a workbook to represent the characters in the story. Children could crayon and cut outlines of these figures and attach them to easily found sticks of various sorts. The workbook might also give the text, the words each character is to assume. Then the children read the text to retell the story, selected children taking parts. This is a more controlled situation. The activity still gives teachers and children a feeling of accomplishment, and there is less uncertainty about the results.

Another point at which there is frequent disagreement between editors and teachers is on the uses of discussion. Many untrained teachers, while firm in their faith, are unsure of the reasons behind what they believe. To have learners ask "why" questions can be unsettling to the teacher who has either avoided or never thought to ask the questions and disturbs the traditional image of the teacher as a person who has all the answers. Such teachers prefer to use concrete questions for which answers can be found in a book. Churches, however, include people who like to ask probing questions. They find it exhilarating to test their beliefs, inquire into biblical meanings, and examine ethical presuppositions. Such people would drop out of a class in which teaching methods left no room for doubt as to the correct answer. In other churches people prefer the security of required interpretations. Classes in such a congregation would reject the inquiry approaches and turn to simpler material in which they could find satisfying answers that did not question any of their own presuppositions.

Chapter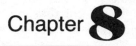

Putting It All Together

It has been stated in these pages that curriculum development is a system made up of a number of components. Several of these have been discussed in separate chapters: a basic design, goals and evaluation, theological and educational assumptions. Other components are the teaching/learning opportunities, resources, and leader development.

From the profile of a parish it becomes possible to state the theological and educational presuppositions that would make some curricular materials more useful than others. The educational level and cultural expectations of the people are other factors involved. By outlining goals and ways of evaluating progress toward them, it is possible to see with some clarity what it is hoped will be accomplished through the materials used.

Teaching/Learning Opportunities: Settings

It would not be realistic to confine a discussion of curriculum materials to those that might be used only on Sunday morning. Some groups never meet at that time. Their classes are held on weekday afternoons or evenings. Youth groups may have both a Sunday morning and a weekday gathering—each different in character. Adult groups may meet at various times through a week or a month. Vacation church school is an additional learning opportunity. Conferences, retreats, and camping provide other occasions for the use of curriculum materials. Roman Catholic materials are frequently designed for use in parochial schools but include a plan for shortened sessions for after-school use by CCD classes. The growing popularity of intergenerational learning events has brought into existence a new set of materials. Parishes have always had intergenerational events, such as bazaars and suppers, in addition to Sunday morning worship, the primary intergenerational event. Many parishes hold special events during Lent or Advent that might include a meal and worship together and study in age-level groups. Now they will find specific help in theme-centered intergenerational material. Many denominations issue special study materials for women's groups with a new theme for each year. Some denominations have similar materials for men's groups. There are also materials for marriage enrichment retreats, premarital conferences, Cursillo, inquirers' classes, baptism and church membership, preparation for first Communion.

One may be surprised at how many learning opportunities there are in any parish. Making a chart will facilitate a quick survey. In one column list all the educational settings, such as women's groups, vacation church school, youth groups, and of course Sunday church school/CCD. Other columns could show when the group meets and for how long, the age level included and the number of attenders. For example:

Educational Setting	Meeting Time	Age Level	Number Attending
Sunday church school	Sunday morning	ages 2 and up	300
Marriage enrichment	Fri.-Sat.; Oct., May	married couples	20 per group

When a committee has completed such a chart, it will have concrete information about the number of learning activities available, the variety of experiences offered, the age span, and the numbers of people involved. The committee will also discover the omissions in the church's program. Is one age level overlooked? Is there a surplus of spiritual life groups? Are there adequate opportunities for couples but not for singles? Are there groups for people with special needs or groups that represent different approaches to Bible study?

Gaps in the chart are not automatic signals to start more groups. The number of groups that a parish can support depends on its size. The chart might suggest the wisdom of developing groups that meet on a short-term basis. In this way a small parish in the course of a year can meet the needs of many people at different times. There is nothing to indicate that people necessarily learn more by attending a class for fifty-two weeks. The important factors are faithfulness in attendance and involvement in the course.

Another possible discovery to be learned from the chart is how unmet needs could be satisfied through interchurch co-operation. For all the talk about ecumenicity, it is rare to find churches of even the same denomination within a community or area pooling their resources to improve teacher training, obtain films, invite resource persons, or in other ways meet specific needs. This lack of cooperation has made congregational attempts to enrich education both provincial and weak.

One of the most fruitful endeavors of this kind in my experience was held among three parishes in a small New England town: United Church of Christ, Roman Catholic, and Episcopal. They cooperated in sponsoring a series of four meetings on baptism. At the first session, a professor from the religion department of a nearby college outlined the historic and biblical development of the rite. On subsequent occasions the group went to each of the churches in turn where a pastor explained that church's theological understandings of the rite and how it is celebrated. The series was so well received that another·one was developed on the theme of the Eucharist. No published material was available for such a course, but a film was obtained, and each pastor presented for study the written order of the rite.

It is necessary to search for material when developing new learning settings, but publishers are beginning to recognize this need. Because these are new learning situations, editors and writers feel less hampered by tradition so that some lively material sometimes results. Look particularly at newer camp, conference, and retreat materials and short-term courses for junior high, high school, and adult classes.

Another implication of an inquiry into the variety of learning settings available is that the Sunday morning or CCD class is only one of many educational possibilities. There is no need to try to accomplish the task in one hour a week. A Sunday session can pick up learnings from other settings and incorporate them, reviewing the previous week's events or introducing coming events. When a study of family begins, a teacher might introduce this by saying, "Some of you went to family camp last summer. Could you share with us what you enjoyed there?" Vacation church school, although in one sense a break from traditional

Sunday patterns, can also be an avenue for review and reinforcement, or it can introduce material to be developed during a fall unit.

Deciding on Groupings

Written curricular material is published on age levels. Many curricula are closely graded with courses corresponding to each school level from one to twelve. Others are on a two-year cycle. These presuppose a teaching setting small enough so that it is necessary to place children of two levels into one class. A third option is a three-year graded cycle. Many churches are so small in membership that they need broadly graded materials that would include children in four or even six grade levels. Such materials are difficult to find. Age level is an important factor but not the only one to consider. Pupil material is written with reference to the ideas that children at a particular age can comprehend. Teacher manuals are designed with pupils at a certain age level in view.

Closely graded materials are among the most substantial, educationally speaking, that can be found. This is especially true of Roman Catholic materials because a whole year's work is contained in one manual. A teacher can do serious advance planning with this material. These materials can be used with adaptations even where there are fewer children. If children in levels one to three are together, the courses for those three grades would be used in successive years on a three-year cycle. Closely graded materials, being designed for larger schools, seem to presuppose (although this may not be a fact) that parishes using such materials are in locations where educational standards are high and parents demand "quality" materials. If a parish does indeed find such materials more challenging than the group-graded materials available, it is possible to adapt them for local use, despite the gap in learning experience between children in grades one and three.

Group-graded materials, whether on a two- or three-year cycle, are intended to help smaller churches. Unfortunately, the amount of help given is dubious. The fact is that small churches do not always have learners neatly distributed into age groups. There may be ten preschoolers, one first grader, six second graders, and three third graders. The disparity makes any attempt at group grading awkward. A teacher will need to meet the needs of the lone child who is at a different grade level than the rest. In this imagined group, for example, the first-grade child would not be able to read as well as could the second and third graders in the class, but the child also would not feel comfortable in a group with preschoolers. At the other end of the age spectrum, a lone ninth grader will not want to associate with a large group of seventh graders and eighth graders.

The solution to this kind of imbalance is to give special attention to a program for the child in the minority. Older children can assist the first grader. The ninth grader can help the teacher by working with younger boys and girls. The material will not tell a teacher how to do this. Developing the skill to make such adaptations comes from a teacher's sensitivity to the individual needs of children.

Alternatively in this situation group-graded materials may give more latitude for meeting the needs of children of mixed ages even in a setting large enough to have closely graded classes. Schools have long known that even within one age level there will be diversities of gifts. A group-graded curriculum may be the solution to this need for some teachers.

Churches needing a broadly graded curriculum that includes up to six grades have had little place to turn. Unfortunately, few publishers of a three-year cycle curriculum use parallel subjects on each level so that a teacher could adapt materials from both levels one to three and four to six.[1] The use of learning centers could be a solution to the need to adapt a curriculum for a small group of learners of varying ages—a sort of one-room schoolhouse approach.

Decisions about grading must be made at the parish level. The groups may shift from year to year because no one can guarantee the same age levels continuously. Material should not be rejected simply because it does not describe itself as being designed for the groupings a parish may have. Examine it with the local situation in mind. Age level may be a less important factor than others, such as theological or educational approach, goals, format, or "teachability."

A Place for Teaching

Whatever material is being considered, the physical setting is an important factor in making it possible to obtain the most from what the material has to offer. If teachers are accustomed to meeting a class around a table where a story is told or there is discussion and some activity work, there will need to be some separation from the sight if not the sound of other classes. When materials suggest the use of projected visual aids, a class will need a corner where this activity will not disturb other groups, unless a church has set aside a gathering place for any group using such materials. Similarly, the use of reference materials may require setting up a corner for those who are working on assignments. Learning hymns or other materials of worship would disturb nearby classes, but space discovered elsewhere in the building would make this possible.

Consider sharing space in such a way that corners are set aside for specific activities. There is no need to put small classes in one large room. Take an example from the one-room schoolhouse and group learners into larger classes with two or more teachers. A visit to a day school class would astonish many Sunday church school teachers who have believed that learning takes place only when pupils are sitting still. The necessity of active participation by the learner is a truism in education today. Consideration of this factor should encourage curriculum planners to welcome materials that call for a variety of methods and not to feel confined because of size or space to certain traditional ways of teaching. Even the financial factor is not overriding. Equipment can be borrowed or minimal equipment bought on a program of budget planning.

Suppose there are several rooms set aside for classes. That does not confine the church school to age groupings and materials based on the number who can be fitted into a room. Instead of designating each room for an age-level class, plan to use each room for an activity: a listening room, an activity center, or a visual aids center. Bring everyone together in a larger gathering room whenever a special resource is available, such as a speaker or film, that might be shared in a larger group.

After questions of space come considerations about equipment. Manuals for preschool teachers frequently include a diagram of how it is hoped the room will be arranged in order for children to engage in a variety of activities. This does not require assembling expensive equipment so much as using imagination for making equipment in less expensive ways than would be the price if bought.

At other age levels filmstrips and slides are frequently suggested. Do not ignore these possibilities. They are widely used in schools. This means that they are not an unusual pleasure for pupils but, rather, that they are a taken-for-granted way of teaching and learning. Frequently the equipment can be borrowed, and inviting the owner to operate the machine might involve someone other than the regular teachers in the program. Tape recorders are now so inexpensive that it should not be difficult to afford one. This is an excellent way to let children record their stories or to tape conversation for use in class. For example, if the minister is conducting Sunday worship during the time a class meets, theological questions from the class could be submitted to the pastor during the week in a taped interview, and the results could be played during the class session. Hymns suggested for learning in the teaching materials can be taped in advance. Film projectors can usually be rented for small fees from a community agency, and home movie cameras frequently are also available.

Resources

Curriculum materials include suggestions for the use of audiovisual equipment because editors know how enriching this can be and how widely available are the materials. However, these are never made so integral a part of the session plan that the class could not be taught without them. They are suggested as additional activities. If you find such suggestions in curriculum material, this does not mean that the curriculum must be rejected for lack of equipment. This could be a stimulus to evaluating the program to see if the use of extra resources might add a dimension for learning.

A teacher who tries to teach with nothing but a teaching manual and a pupil book is either extremely inventive or totally innocent. Professional teachers assume that they will have teaching helps of all kinds. This is why the curriculum materials one examines will include lists of books, tapes, records, and visual aids. As in the case of equipment, the use of resources is not essential, but it can increase the effectiveness of one's work immeasurably.

For this reason, the collection and dissemination of resources can be regarded as one of the essential elements in the total system called religious education. Teachers may think that because there are only forty-five to sixty minutes with a class, this extra material is not necessary. To be sure, only a minimal amount of food is needed to sustain life, very few clothes are needed for warmth, and lives could be lived without any of the cultural events that civilizations have developed through the arts, music, and literature, yet life is fuller for these enrichments. No one can make the most of a curriculum without planning to acquire some supplementary resources. These add variety for teacher and learner, increase the available methods of teaching, offer several avenues through which to learn, and build up a collection of materials that will be useful for years to come. Unlike many of the basic series of courses that become outdated as soon as the next cycle appears, these materials can be used continually and are adaptable across age levels. They can be utilized for preclass browsing or as an extra activity for the child who finishes assignments quickly. They can be loaned to families for at-home use and be used in summer programs.

There is no need to be overwhelmed by the number of resources suggested. Ask teachers to examine their manuals and list those resources that seem most essential for fully utilizing the materials. Ask them to make up a second list of desirable but not necessary resources. Set aside a budget item each year for purchasing such resources. Give priority to those materials that can be rotated among the most people. In a few years, a parish will have a valuable resource center.

Plan also to stock supplies such as papers, paints, and other activity materials suggested in the teacher's manual. One will find that an accumulation of such basic materials costs less than would some of the auxiliary teaching materials offered by publishers and will be more flexible. Materials such as boxes, ribbons, or used magazines can be collected from homes. Skilled teachers have long known how to accumulate such resources, and efficient helpers have learned how to shelve and catalogue them in a room or closet to be readily available for teaching use.

Publishers of curriculum material have lists of resources for sale, and churches should seriously consider their own needs before ordering, for these resources can become expensive. One will need to decide how essential a pupil workbook is for teaching. These may hold children's interest or add to knowledge in such a way as to seem worth buying in addition to or in place of less structured activities. A teaching packet usually contains a number of aids: large pictures, filmstrip, poster, and group activities. One will want to be sure that its usefulness is worth the price. If it is ordered, ensure its use beyond the time that it ties in with a specific class need by later filing the components under separate headings. Then one will not need to order the same packet the second time the cycle comes around.

There may also be available a "take-home" sheet for the pupil. Its usefulness varies. Ask the questions "Why are the children taking this home? How does it enhance their religious education through the family?" The leaflet may include homework or reinforce the class session by reviewing materials or be a link with parents by addressing some material to them. Under such circumstances it could be a valuable part of the interaction between church and family. A take-home paper could also be useful if sent to absentees with the memo "We missed you in class. Hope to see you soon." Unfortunately, as an examination of most church school closets will reveal, this seldom happens. Scores of unused leaflets pile up on the shelves. Someone could have mailed out leaflets at the close of class, but nobody thought to do so. One might decide that the take-home paper is in fact useful but that fewer copies are needed, making sure that these are mailed each week.

A Teachable Curriculum

What makes a course of study teachable? Teachers will say that they look at the format. This is the makeup of the teacher's book. In order to be inviting, a book must have wide margins and the print must be attractively placed. If it does not have illustrations, there must be varieties of typeface, bold and italics, capitals and lowercase letters, indentations, and spacings that add a visual interest to each page. This attractiveness is inviting to the reader.

A course of study is made teachable when, in addition to attractive format, the outline of each session is carefully constructed. A teacher wants the objectives to be clearly stated at the beginning—perhaps in a section set apart in a box. The next expectation is that a brief outline of the session be given, step by step, perhaps with suggested time frames.

The next needed information is a listing of materials and resources to be assembled. This is usually entitled "Getting Ready for the Session," and it should be so arranged that the teacher sees clearly each activity for which preparation needs to be made. For example, "The class will need Bibles, 8" x 11" manila paper, paste, and magazines from which to obtain pictures"; or "You will want to look up the following references in your Bible in order to be able to read them in class"; or "If you are planning to have the minister explain the service to the class, be sure that the invitation has been given in advance and the minister knows when to arrive at the classroom." Such a list cues the teacher into supplies needed, teaching preparation expected, and resource persons to be notified.

Finally, there needs to be a running description of how the session can progress. This will include conversation and discussion questions and a clear description of activities. If teachers are to be encouraged to explore a variety of methods, each one needs to be carefully explained, with illustrations, in order to develop confidence. This is not an easy form of writing, but popular magazines manage to do it, and teacher manuals must.

A teachable manual also includes introductory sections that will outline the course, describe both the general and religious development of children at that age level, give biblical and theological background for material being taught, list needed resources, and describe how to carry out activities. It must be admitted that many teachers will skip these sections and proceed immediately to the plans for the first session unless they are skillfully guided to read this material. Many teachers really need to learn about child development or biblical background. Theoretically this introductory section increases the teachability of the manual; practically it may not. But this is no reason for omitting it. Ways can be found to make the contents effective.

The pupil book is another part of the "teachable" curriculum. Few publishers prepare first Bible reading books for beginning readers, although some such books are available through regular book channels. These pupil books must meet the criteria of other children's books: liveliness in storytelling and attractiveness of illustration. Most curriculum series include attractive children's books that can form a core library collection. Books for adolescents, however, are in marked contrast to the children's books. They have fewer illustrations, use little color, and pay scant attention to format that invites the attention of the reader. Most astonishingly, adult religious education materials are dull beyond description. Curiously, the children's teacher's book, which also is intended for use by adults, is deliberately designed to be attractive. But the materials used by *other* adults in *their* classes, as well as materials for teachers of youth and adults, ignore completely such canons of "teachability." Publishers of the Uniform Lesson Series outlines seem to be more prone to this than do others. The designers of adult materials try to use boldface headings, indented block paragraphs, and wide margins to give relief to the eye, but this is little enough. Anyone who examines a wide variety of curriculum materials soon concludes that Protestant adult curriculum is so set in a traditional mold that no one even realizes it could be different.

When it comes to "teachable" material, by the definitions that teachers use, independent publishers in general seem to do a better job than do denominational publishers, with general textbook houses doing the best job. The production of attractively designed material cannot be entirely a financial matter (the more attractive it is does not necessarily mean the more expensive it is), although a large volume of production tends to keep down the cost per unit for the independent publishers. The most recent denominational materials have been much improved in the use of color and illustrations.

People who look for aesthetically satisfying art in curriculum materials will often be disappointed. Some books include reproductions of classical and modern art as illustrations in books for teachers and older learners.[2] Few use contemporary style illustrations. Children's trade books have a kind of illustration that portrays "everyperson," a figure with whom any reader can identify. Little of this is to be found in religious education material, which, instead, tries to be "realistic." Designers are now making good use of photo illustration, which is a contemporary way of being realistic without being sentimental.

On the whole, curriculum materials show a contemporary use of print but lag behind general publishing in the use of illustration. In many churches this difference will not be noticed, but it speaks to the cultural limitations of religious educational publishing work.

When the varied settings and occasions for using religious education materials, the possible age-level combinations, and the use of building, equipment, and resources are put together, there are broad possibilities for an effective teaching program. As a final criterion, look carefully at the attractiveness of the material. Appearance is no substitute for substantive content, but it is essential if that content is to be usable.

Chapter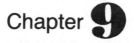

A Concluding Word

Curriculum materials and the curriculum have been almost synonymous terms in religious education until recently. This has not been the case in general education, where, in any given subject, the graded courses of study materials are but one element in the teaching plan. Such a system presupposes teachers who are professionally trained and paid and for whom *planning* to teach is as essential as the teaching period itself. The teacher's planbook has been a key element in the process.

Many teachers in Sunday church schools and CCD classes also plan for each teaching session, but not all consider this to be an integral part of the process. Some are recruited on the assurance that the work will not require much of their time. They willingly offer an hour a week but have no clear plan for structuring preparatory time. Publishers bend their efforts toward developing easily used materials for such teachers. A lively teacher who has rapport with a class can use these materials to provide a session that gives assurance, a sense of community, and the feeling that the teacher cares. Essentially most such classes are places where adults who are teachers share their faith with class members. The system breaks down if the teacher has little to share and can only repeat what the book suggests.

Contrary to the fondest hopes of publishers, editors, writers, judicatory resource persons, pastors, and others in the local church, "improved" teaching materials will not much alter the teaching pattern. Only "improved" teachers will provide better teaching.

Those who recruit teachers will need to stop asking for the minimum amount of time. They need to be honest by admitting the indubitable fact that preparation is essential to good teaching. They would be even more helpful if they persuaded prospective teachers that some time learning *how* to prepare would make further preparation simpler. Who is to do this?

This may be a task that teachers can work on together in departmental groups or as a whole group. One among them could be coordinator—not necessarily the one who has been teaching longest but the one most skilled in planning. A pastor, superintendent, or member of the church who teaches school might be such a coordinator. The task is to take teachers through planning steps, each using the teaching manual provided.

First they will need to clarify objectives for the year, the quarter, or the unit. Then they will want to read material in their teaching book that describes the learner. This information will be tested as they work with their own classes. Next they will want to read and discuss introductory material about the course content. This will lead to the consideration of methods used to convey this content to learners in order to achieve stated objectives.

Now they are ready to see the overall plan for each session, an order that usually does not change much from lesson to lesson. This survey of the teacher's book, session by session, will give teachers an opportunity to note where they might want to plan for special features at particular times.

With such an overview, which will require several hours, teachers can enter the classroom for the first session secure in the knowledge that the course is within their comprehension. They can modify it week by week in accordance with the needs of their pupils, the resources available, and their own teaching capabilities, but they need never be uncertain as to what they will do. This overall preparation gives any teacher a technique for approaching the task which can be followed without outside guidance after the initial practice session.

Sometimes teachers simply need reassurance—to have someone ask at the end of a session how things went or to phone later in the day to say something helpful about the session. They need the kind of recognition that can be given through an annual dedication service that includes a pledge by the congregation to assist in the process of nurture and education. They like being the honored person at coffee hour one Sunday and having a thank-you dinner either at the beginning or end of the teaching year. They would like to be asked what kind of help they need, rather than being told that a meeting will be held for their benefit.

People take risks only when they feel secure, and church teachers will try new methods, resources, or materials only after they have developed some feeling about their own capabilities and received some assurances that they are doing well. These minimal steps will improve teaching.

A parish-developed curriculum, in which materials are chosen to fit a theme and teaching outlines are left to be enriched through teacher initiative, requires for its effectiveness teachers who already feel assured of their own skills and have a sense of adventure. These people will probably be involved in the choice of themes and units as well as in searching for resources. Their cooperation and continuing enthusiasm are essential if such an approach is to flourish. The alternative would be the fading of a hope with the realization that the task was more than anyone could spend time fulfilling. Developing a curriculum is a time-consuming project.

If there are not many people willing to do even minimal preparation for teaching, it would be better to plan for fewer teachers and larger classes. Most Sunday church schools, if not CCD classes, are overstaffed. This happens because of the mistaken notion that an insecure teacher who cannot handle a larger group is able to teach a few children. Sometimes boys and girls are placed in separate classes under the illusion that girls are easier to "handle" than are boys. Discipline is usually a teacher problem, not a pupil or curriculum problem. Skilled teaching is the only solution, unless, as sometimes happens, there is indeed a disruptive child in the group who will require special attention.

Stronger teaching could be obtained through team teaching because two people would reinforce one another, each could use individual skills while trying out new skills, and if one were absent, the other would give continuity to the class. But the tradition of one teacher to one class in one room (or corner of a large room) is so strong that the idea is difficult to implement. Team teaching could be both more efficient and more effective.

When anyone hears the word "curriculum," images of printed materials come to mind, along with all the auxiliary helps that are offered. But, in fact, superimposed on any picture of curriculum must be the faces of those who will teach. The two are inseparable. All materials are written with these persons in mind.

The systems approach to curriculum planning keeps a number of factors in balance. All the people involved define the goals and set up ways for evaluation. Then they are in a position to describe and define the theological and educational presuppositions on which their religious education program should rest. Knowing both parish and community, with their learning needs and potential, the educational task force can sketch out learning experiences and begin to collect resources. Finally, the teachers, who presumably have been part of the foregoing process insofar as they wished to be, continue the process through their own development for more effective teaching.

The demand for curricular materials that are responsive to the particular needs of a congregation is a growing one. The present need is for a continuance of the effort to place at the disposal of local planners instruments through which they can with some ease analyze their situations and their requirements. This analysis will enable congregations to explore potential materials with some discernment. Examination copies, available through most publishers, are a help in such exploration and planning. Local church educational planners are developing into critical consumers. The challenge to respond to more specifically expressed needs could lead to greater creativity on the part of publishers.[1]

This stage in curriculum development has been a long time coming. It holds dangers both for denominations with money invested in new programs and for parishes attempting a degree of involvement in curriculum construction that they have not tackled before. But out of it will come new directions, new forms and resources for teaching, and a deeper attention to fulfilling seriously the church's teaching function.

Appendix I

An Evaluation Checklist for Use When Choosing Curriculum Materials

Look carefully at the teacher's book

Goals
- What are the stated goals?
- Are they similar to the goals you have set for teaching/learning?
- Are they specific enough so that you can know when you have accomplished them?

Content
- Is the material what you need for study this year?
- Does the biblical material reflect an acceptable understanding of biblical interpretation?
- Is the biblical content appropriate for the learners at the age at which they will be using it?
- Is the interpretation of the biblical material appropriate for the age at which it will be used? (Not too simple for older learners or too abstract for younger learners.)
- Does the material help learners understand what it means to be part of the Christian community—its worship, history, beliefs, structure, mission?

Life Experience
- How does the material interpret the meaning of the Christian life? To what extent is this in agreement with the understanding you have set in your presuppositions?
- How does the material relate Christian living to biblical learning?

- Does the material give opportunities to practice and reflect upon actions that express a Christian life-style? Be specific.
- How does the material relate personal religious living to living in family, school, community, world, and environment?
- How does the material foster ecumenical understanding and an understanding of non-Christian religious groups?

Teaching the Course

- Is the format of the book attractive?
- Is each session clearly outlined so that a teacher can easily understand the steps for teaching? Are there particular features that help the teacher grasp the outline?
- What methods for teaching are suggested? With which of these are the teachers comfortable? Which new ones could be easily learned?
- Are instructions for activities clear and easy to follow?
- What resources are suggested for use beyond those in the book? Which of these are essential? Which could be easily obtained?
- Does the course book include helpful material about the age and learning levels of those in the class?
- Is there background material about the content so that teachers' information will be enriched?

Look carefully at the pupil material

Reading book

- Is it attractively illustrated (from a child's viewpoint)?
- Is the print easy to read for a child?
- Would the style and language attract a child's interest?
- Is the story within a child's understanding?

Workbook

- Would the exercises be interesting to children?
- Are they too difficult? too easy? Explain.
- Would they enrich the understanding of the lesson? How?
- Would they be helpful enough for the cost involved? (Or would it be better to develop activities specifically for the class?)

Activity packet

- Which activities are most likely to be used? How often?
- Critically speaking, what is the quality of each item: picture, filmslip, poster, and so on?

- Will children find the suggested activities useful, or could similar activities be constructed with little effort and less expense?

Take-home paper

- What is the purpose of this paper as evidenced by its design and content?
- Would it reinforce the lesson for use at home?
- Would it enrich the material used in class?
- Would it be a link between absentees and the class?
- How valuable would it be as a contact with the families of children present in class? of those who were absent?
- Is it worth the price? Why or why not?

Look at the overall design of the total curriculum

- What are the goals over a six-, eight- or twelve-year span?
- List the basic content of each unit of the twelve-year span.
- Note the "flow" of the material.

How is biblical material used: topically? chronologically? other? What are the advantages/disadvantages of this design?

Where do repetitions of material occur? Do these reinforce learning? deepen insights? fill space?

Are units planned for seasonal emphases? Are these useful?

Are the required resources within the budget of your congregation? Are they within the teaching skills of your teachers?

Is there space for additions or substitutions for special studies without disrupting the pattern (such as missions project, worship, stewardship, ecumenical study)?

Concluding question

Weighing the advantages and disadvantages, would this be the most useful curriculum package for your parish now? State reasons.

Appendix II

Curriculum Publishers

African Methodist Episcopal Church, Department of Christian Education, 500 Eighth Avenue, S., Nashville, TN 37203. Group-graded, preschool to adult. Uniform Lesson Series outlines.

African Methodist Episcopal Zion Church, Department of Christian Education Literature, Box 31045, Charlotte, NC 28230. Three-year group-graded, preschool to adult. Uniform Lesson Series outlines, adult.

American Baptist Churches in the U.S.A., Board of Educational Ministries, Valley Forge, PA 19481. Bible and Life curriculum, 2-year graded materials, kindergarten through grade 6; 3-year graded, grades 7 through 12. Adult Elective series. Uniform Lesson Series outlines, adult, senior high, junior high. Also *Living the Word* (see separate listing for CE:SA).

Anglican Church of Canada, Church House, 600 Jarvis Street, Toronto, Ontario, M4Y 2J6, Canada. Group-graded curriculum, preschool through grade 12, adult.

Argus Communications, Dept. 50, Box 7000, Allen, TX 75002. High school, adult materials on these topics: Bible, world religions, moral values.

Assemblies of God, Gospel Publishing House, 1445 Booneville Avenue, Springfield, MO 65802. Two-year group-graded materials, preschool through adults; adult electives.

Augsburg Publishing House, 426 S. Fifth Street, Box 1209, Minneapolis, MN 55440. Proclaim series: closely graded, home nursery through grade 9; confirmation/junior high, high school, adult. Alleluia series: 2-year group-graded, music/arts/ worship oriented. Vacation church school materials. American Lutheran Church.

Ave Maria Press, Notre Dame, IN 46556. High school electives: "Faith and You," "Jesus and You," and so on.

Behrman House Inc., 1261 Broadway, New York, NY 10001. 2-year graded, kindergarten through adult: Bible, Jewish history and values.

Benziger, Bruce & Glencoe, Inc., 17337 Ventura Boulevard, Encino, CA 91316. Closely graded, grades 1 through 8. Sacramental preparation. For CCD and schools.

Board of Parish Education, 2900 Queen Lane, Philadelphia, PA 19129. Units of study, closely or group-graded, nursery through grade 6. Junior high catechetical. Elective units for grades 10 through 12 and adults. Vacation church school. Lutheran Church in America.

Wm. C. Brown Group. Religious Education Division, 2460 Kerper Boulevard, Dubuque, IA 52001. 2-year preschool cycle; closely graded, grades 1 through 9; electives for junior high, high school. Sacramental preparation.

Christian Education: Shared Approaches (CE:SA). Order through the cooperating denominational publishing houses: American Baptist Churches in the U.S.A., Valley Forge, PA 19481; Christian Board of Publication (Disciples of Christ), Box 179, St. Louis, MO 63166; Brethren Press (Church of the Brethren), 1451 Dundee Avenue, Elgin, IL 60120; Cumberland Presbyterian Resource Center (Cumberland Presbyterian Church), 1978 Union Avenue, Memphis, TN 38104; UCBHM Division of Publication (The Episcopal Church and United Church of Christ), 132 W. 31st. Street, New York, NY 10001; Covenant Press (The Evangelical Covenant Church), 3200 W. Foster Avenue, Chicago 60625; The Moravian Church, North, 5 W. Market Street, Bethlehem, PA 18018; The Moravian Church, South, Drawer Y, Winston-Salem, NC 27108; Presbyterian Publications (The Presbyterian Church in Canada), 52 Wynford Drive, Don Mills, Ontario M3C 1J8; Materials Distribution Service (Presbyterian Church in the US and The Reformed Church in America), 341 Ponce de Leon Avenue, NE, Atlanta, GA 30365; CANEC Publishing and Supply House (United Church of Canada), 47 Coldwater Road, Don Mills, Ontario M3B 1Y9; Curriculum Services UPCUSA (United Presbyterian

Church, U.S.A.), Box 868-William Penn Annex, Philadelphia, PA 19105. Four approaches. *Knowing the Word,* Children's Bible Series: 2-year preschool, 3-year graded, kindergarten through grade 6, Uniform Lesson Series outlines for youth and adults. *Interpreting the Word,* 2-year graded, kindergarten through grade 5; 3-year graded, grades 6 through 8; older youth/adult. *Living the Word,* 2-year graded, birth through grade 7; 3-year graded, grades 7 through 12; adult. Also the Youth Elect series for younger and older youth; congregational life experiences and intergenerational materials. *Doing the Word,* materials from denominational publishers and Friendship Press (see separate listing).

Christian Methodist Episcopal Church, Department of Christian Education, 1474 Humber Street, Memphis, TN 38101. 3-year graded, nursery through adult. Uniform Lesson Series outlines.

Christian Reformed Church, Board of Publication, 2850 Kalamazoo Avenue, SE, Grand Rapids, MI 49560. The Bible Way curriculum: Nursery, 2-year graded, kindergarten through grade 10. Core courses and electives for young adults; electives for adults; special education materials.

Concordia Publishing House, 3558 S. Jefferson Avenue, St. Louis, MO 63118. Nursery, 2-year graded, kindergarten through grade 8. High school and adult electives. Weekday, parochial school, vacation church school, special education. Lutheran Church, Missouri Synod.

David C. Cook Publishing Co., 850 N. Grove Avenue, Elgin, IL 60120. 2-year graded, nursery through grade 6, 3-year graded for grades 7 through 12. Senior high electives; young adult "Lifestyle"; Uniform Lesson Series outlines, adult; adult electives.

The Educational Center, 6357 Clayton Road, St. Louis, MO 63117. Centerquest curriculum: 2-year graded, kindergarten through grade 3; 3-year graded, grades 4 through 12; adult. Teaching correlated with trade books centering on relationships. Jungian-oriented elective courses, grade 7 through adults.

Free Methodist Publishing House, 999 College Avenue, Winona Lake, IN 46590. Aldersgate curriculum: 2-year graded preschool; 3-year graded, grades 1 through 12. Uniform Lesson Series outlines, adults; adult electives. A cooperative curriculum of churches within the Wesleyan tradition, including the Wesleyan Church, Marion, IN. The Missionary Church, Ft. Wayne, IN; The Churches of Christ in Christian Union, Circleville, OH; the Evangelical Friends Alliance; and the Nazarene Church (see separate listing) which publishes additional material for its constituency. Free Methodist Church.

Friendship Press, Distributing Office, 7820 Reading Road, Box 37844, Cincinnati, OH 45237. New materials each year on two annual themes: the church in North America and the church overseas. Children, youth, adults. Also available through denominational offices.

Friendship General Conference, 1520-B Race Street, Philadelphia, PA 19102. Group-graded materials, preschool through adults.

Gospel Light Pub. Co., 2300 Knoll Drive, Ventura, CA 93003. *Living the Word:* preschool; 2-year graded, grades 1 through 8; grade 9, grades 10 through 12.

Loyola University Press, 3441 N. Ashland Avenue, Chicago, IL 60657. Christ Our Life curriculum: closely graded, grades 1 through 8 and confirmation. For CCD and schools.

Mennonite Church, 616 Walnut Avenue, Scottdale, PA 15683. Foundation series for children: 2-year graded, birth through grade 8. Used also by the Mennonite Church (KS), Brethren in Christ, and, cooperatively, by the Church of the Brethren.

Media Action Research Center, Suite 1370, 475 Riverside Drive, New York, NY 10115. *Growing with Television:* 3-year graded, grades 1 through adult. Four units of study. Order through denominational publishing houses.

Morehouse-Barlow Co., Inc., 78 Danbury Road, Wilton, CT 06897. Sacramental preparation (Episcopal); stewardship, grades 7 through 11; parenting.

National Baptist Sunday Board, 330 Charlotte Avenue, Nashville, TN 37201. 3-year graded, preschool through grade 12, young adult, adult. Uniform Lesson Series outlines.

Nazarene Publishing House, Box 527, Kansas City, MO 64141. Group-graded, nursery through adults. Uniform Lesson Series outlines. Cooperates in Aldersgate materials.

Our Sunday Visitor, Inc., Religious Education Department, Noll Plaza, Huntington, IN 46750. Closely graded, kindergarten through grade 8. Sacramental preparation.

Paulist Press, 545 Island Road, Ramsey, NJ 07446. Preschool, elementary, high school, and adult electives. Sacramental preparation. Family (intergenerational) units.

William H. Sadlier Inc., 11 Park Place, New York, NY 10007. Closely graded, kindergarten through grade 8. Sacramental preparation; summer programs.

St. Mary's Press, Terrace Heights, Winona, MN 55987. High school electives; human development units.

St. Vladimir's Press, Crestwood, NY 10707. Orthodox Christian Education Program: 3-year graded, preschool through adult; biblically, liturgically, tradition-oriented. Cooperatively by several Eastern Orthodox churches.

Scripture Press Publications, Inc., 1825 College Avenue, Wheaton, IL 60187. Group-graded, 2 years of age through grade 12, on a 2- or 3-year cycle. High school and adult electives; special education.

Silver Burdett Co., Educational/Religious Sales, 250 James Street, Morristown, NJ 07960. Preschool; closely graded, grades 1 through 8; for CCD and schools. A 4-year high school program; sacramental programs.

Southern Baptist Sunday School Board, SBC Materials Services Department, 127 Ninth Avenue, N., Nashville, TN 37234. Preschool, 3-year graded, grades 1 through 12. Uniform Lesson Series outlines, adults. Electives for youth and adults.

Standard Publishing, 8121 Hamilton Avenue, Cincinnati, OH 45231. Preschool, 2-year graded, grades 1 through 6; 3-year graded, grades 7 through 10; adult. Uniform Lesson Series outlines, special education materials.

Twenty-Third Publications, Inc., 185 Willow Street, Box 180, Mystic, CT 06355. Electives, grades 7 through 12; sacramental programs; leadership development; summer.

Union of American Hebrew Congregations, 838 Fifth Avenue, New York, NY 10021. 3-year group-graded, grades 1 through 12, adult. Bible, history, tradition.

Unitarian-Universalist Curriculum Development Office, 25 Beacon Street, Boston, MA 02108. Multi-media project kits, broadly graded, kindergarten through adults. All materials and resources needed for teaching a unit.

United Methodist Church, Discipleship Resources, 1908 Grand Avenue and 1001 19th Avenue, S., Box 840, Nashville, TN 37202. Children's Bible studies: 2-year graded, grades 1 through 6; 3-year graded, grades 7 through 12. High school and adult electives. Uniform Lesson Series outlines. Vacation church school materials.

Warner Press Inc., 1200 E. Fifth Street, Box 2499, Anderson, IN 46011. Group-graded, preschool through grade 12. Uniform Lesson Series outlines, adults. Church of God.

Winston Press, 430 Oak Grove, Minneapolis, MN 55403. Joy series, preschool through grade 8; Infinity series, high school: heritage and moral development units. Special resources for Episcopal and Lutheran programs.

Urban Ministries Inc., 9917 S. Green Street, Chicago, IL 60643. Emphasizes the black experience. Three-year graded, preschool through adult. Uniform Lesson Series outlines.

Curriculum Guides

Guide to Curriculum Choice (Elgin, Ill.: Brethren Press, 1981). Published for Joint Educational Development. Order through denominational publishing houses.

Christian Educational Catalogue, ed., Ruth Gordon Cheney (New York: The Seabury Press, Inc., 1981).

Curriculum Resources

American Bible Society, 1865 Broadway, New York, NY 10023. Bibles and Bible portions in several versions for all ages.

Anti-Defamation League of B'nai B'rith, 823 United Nations Plaza, New York, NY 10017. Books, pamphlets, audiovisuals.

Griggs Educational Resources, Abingdon Press. Order through Cokesbury regional centers. Bible, church year units, other resources.

Multimedia kits, John and Mary Harrell, Box 9006, Berkeley, CA 94709. Kits for seasons of the Christian year.

National Catholic Reporter, Box 281, Kansas City, MO 64161. Cassette program for adults.

National Teacher Education Project, 7214 East Granada Road, Scottsdale, AZ 85257. Multimedia units, grades 4 through 8; cassettes and filmstrips for leader development.

A Guide to Biblical Resources, Kendig Brubaker Cully and Iris V. Cully (Wilton, Conn.: Morehouse-Barlow Co., Inc., 1981). Units and resources for all ages are discussed.

Serendipity House, Box 7661, Colorado Springs, CO 80933. Multimedia courses, junior high through adults.

Privately Published Curricula

Basic Bible study for adults. Participating churches usually pay a fee in addition to purchasing materials.

The Bethel Series, Box 5305, Madison, WI 53705
The Kerygma Program, Room 2217, 300 Mt. Lebanon Boulevard, Pittsburgh, PA 15234.
Trinity Bible Studies, Box 25101, Dallas, TX 75225
Living The Good News, Episcopal Diocese of Colorado, 600 Gilpin Street, Denver, CO 81218. Group-graded, based on the 3-year lectionary cycle. A form of uniform lessons.

Notes

Chapter 1

[1] Examples: Ralph Earle, comp., *Peloubet's Notes* (Grand Rapids, Mich.: Baker Book House); Frank S. Mead, ed., *Tarbell's Teacher Guide* (Old Tappan, N.J.: Fleming H. Revell, Co.); James Reapsome, *Rozell's Complete Lessons* (Grand Rapids, Mich.: The Zondervan Corp.); Horace B. Weaver, ed., *International Lesson Annual* (Nashville: Abingdon Press).

[2] The most extensive lists seem to be found in the catalogues of the United Methodist Church (specifically, the *Planbook for Adults*), the Lutheran·Church in America, and the Southern Baptist Sunday School Board. See also the *Resource Guide for Adult Religious Education*, comp. Mary Reed Newland (Kansas City, Mo.: National Catholic Reporter Publishing Co., Inc., 1974).

[3] The curriculum catalogue of the Lutheran Church in America offers a curriculum planning guide for parishes. Age level courses are developed in units on various themes, and parishes are invited to plan the year's course of study by choosing among those courses offered. *Developing the Congregation's Educational Program* (Philadelphia: The Westminster Press, The Geneva Press, 1976), published for Christian Education: Shared Approaches, includes a guide to educational materials selection on page 39.

Chapter 2

[1] Such curricula have included the Seabury Series (out-of-print) and the *Time for Living Series* (out-of-print). The Character Research Project for many years produced a character-education curriculum that churches contracted to use. Presently the Educational Center (6357 Clayton Road, St. Louis, MO 63117) publishes experience-oriented curriculum and a Jungian-oriented adult series.

[2] The largest independent Protestant publishers are David C. Cook Publishing Co., Scripture Press Publications, Inc., Gospel Light Pub. Co., and Standard Publishing.

[3] Curricula from the 1960s included the *Covenant Life Curriculum* (Presbyterian Church in the U.S.), the *Christian Life Curriculum* (Christian Church [Disciples of Christ] and American Baptist Churches in the U.S.A.), United Church Press curriculum, *Christian Faith and Action* (United Presbyterian), and that of the Lutheran Church of America.

[4] The partner denominations of Joint Educational Development are the Christian Church (Disciples of Christ), Church of the Brethren, Cumberland Presbyterian Church, the Episcopal Church, Evangelical Covenant Church, the Mo-

121

ravian Church, Presbyterian Church in Canada, Presbyterian Church in the U.S., the Reformed Church in America, United Church of Canada, United Church of Christ, and the United Presbyterian Church, U.S.A. Conversations are in process with two additional denominations.

[5] This period is well described in *Biblical Interpretations in Religious Education* by Mary C. Boys (Birmingham, Ala.: Religious Education Press, 1980).

[6] While the goals will remain the same, the present *Knowing the Word* materials have been replaced by the *Children's Bible Series* developed by a committee under the Division of Education and Ministry of the National Council of Churches. The United Methodist Church has an equivalent series titled *Children's Bible Studies*.

[7] These stages with reference to Christian education are discussed in my book, *Christian Child Development* (New York: Harper & Row Publishers, Inc., 1979.)

[8] For example, the themes for 1982-1983 were "People of the Pacific Islands" and "Pilgrimage of Faith: Oneness in Christ."

[9] These guides are *Planning the Church's Educational Program, Developing the Congregation's Educational Program,* and *Creating the Congregation's Educational Program.*

[10] The David C. Cook Publishing Co. materials try to concentrate on biblical understanding and application, allowing for theological interpretations by the users. Standard materials have a fundamentalist theological emphasis as do those of Gospel Light Pub. Co. and Scripture Press Publications, Inc.

[11] Entitled *The Orthodox Christian Education Program,* these materials are edited by Constance Tarasar and published by St. Vladimir's Seminary Press.

Chapter 3

[1] These originally mimeographed materials now have been condensed in the *Leader Manual for CE:SA* and four approach manuals, one for each of the four curricular options: *Knowing the Word, Interpreting the Word, Living the Word,* and *Doing the Word.*

[2] The *Church's Teaching Series* volumes were foundational to the Seabury Series curriculum in the 1950s. The *Yearbooks in Christian Education,* published by the Lutheran Church in America, have a broader purpose. The basic Methodist document is *Foundations for Teaching and Learning in the United Methodist Church.* Roman Catholics turn to the Declaration on Christian Education from the Documents of Vatican II and *To Teach as Jesus Taught* from the United States Catholic Conference.

[3] This is a service offered by the David C. Cook Publishing Co.

Chapter 4

[1] These studies include Daniel J. Levinson *et al., Seasons of a Man's Life* (New York: Alfred A. Knopf, Inc., 1978); Gail Sheehy, *Passages* (New York: E. P. Dutton, 1977); and the pioneering studies on the development of the healthy personality by Erik H. Erikson. New contributions are coming from the Project on Faith Development in the Adult Life Cycle, headed by Kenneth Stokes under the auspices of the Religious Education Association. This is expected to result in volumes to be published by William H. Sadlier, Inc.

[2] There are helpful charts and fill-in pages in *Developing the Congregation's Educational Program,* noted in Chapter 1, footnote 3.

[3] See the *Alleluia Series* (Minneapolis: Augsburg Publishing House) for teaching about worship, including careful attention to hymns and other musical forms.

Chapter 5

[1] *Christian Faith and Action,* published by the United Presbyterian Church in the U.S.A. Board of Christian Education, Philadelphia, Pa.

[2] Bernard E. Michel, *Knowing the Word* (Philadelphia: The Westminster Press, The Geneva Press, 1977), p. 7.

[3] John C. Purdy, *Interpreting the Word* (Philadelphia: The Westminster Press, The Geneva Press, 1977), p. 7.

[4] Guin Ream Tuckett, *Living the Word* (St. Louis: Christian Board of Publication, 1977), p. 12.

[5] Introductory material, David C. Cook Publishing Co.'s *Bible-in-Life* chart in the 1980 catalog.

[6] *The Church's Educational Ministry: A Curriculum Plan*, the work of the Cooperative Curriculum Project (St. Louis: The Bethany Press, 1965).

[7] Benjamin S. Bloom and David Krathwohl, *Taxonomy of Educational Objectives*, 2 vols. (New York: Longman, Inc., 1977).

[8] National Council of Churches, *Tools of Curriculum Development for the Church's Educational Ministry* (Anderson, Ind.: Warner Press, Inc., 1976), p. 33.

[9] Sr. Marie de la Cruz Aymes and Francis S. Buckley, "God Loves Me" in *Lord of Life* (Encino, Calif.: Benziger, Bruce & Glencoe, Inc.), p. 13.

[10] _____, "Grow in God's Love" in *The Word Is Life*, grade 2, 2nd. ed., (New York: William H. Sadlier, Inc., 1980).

[11] Curriculum catalogue, 1980-81 (Cincinnati: Standard Publishing, 1980), p. 2.

[12] This is the model outlined in the planning books for Joint Educational Development. See chapter 2, footnote 9.

Chapter 6

[1] "Verbal inspiration of the Bible" is the first of the five fundamentals. The list was given in a packet of materials issued by the company.

[2] *Leader Manual*, p. 49.

[3] William A. Beardslee, *Literary Criticism of the New Testament* (Philadelphia: Fortress Press, 1970); Edgar V. McKnight, *What Is Form Criticism?* ed. Dan O. Via, Jr. (Philadelphia: Fortress Press, 1969); Norman Perrin, *What Is Redaction Criticism?* (Philadelphia: Fortress Press, 1969); and Daniel Patte, *What Is Structural Exegesis?* (Philadelphia: Fortress Press, 1976). There is a parallel series on the Old Testament.

[4] This is the view of John H. Westerhoff, III, outlined in his book *Will Our Children Have Faith?* (New York: The Seabury Press, Inc., 1976).

Chapter 7

[1] An easy way of getting into his thought is found in the small paperback, Jean Piaget, *Six Psychological Studies*, ed. David Elkind, trans. Anita Tenzer (New York: Random House, Inc., 1968); also Jean Piaget and Barbel Inhelder, *The Psychology of the Child*, trans. Helen Weaver (New York: Basic Books, Inc., Publishers, 1969).

[2] Erikson first outlined these stages in Erik H. Erikson, *Childhood & Society* (New York: W. W. Norton & Co., Inc., 1950).

[3] Jean Piaget, *The Moral Judgment of the Child* (New York: The Free Press, 1932).

[4] Ronald Goldman carried out basic research included in his book *Religious Thinking from Childhood to Adolescence* (New York: The Seabury Press, Inc., 1968).

[5] *Interpreting the Word* and *Living the Word* materials incorporate this as an alternative learning procedure.

[6] Examples of such materials are Mary Reed Newland, comp., *The Resource Guide for Adult Religious Education* (Kansas City, Mo.: National Catholic Reporter Publishing Co., Inc., 1974); Leon McKenzie, *Creative Learning for Adults* (Mystic, Conn.: Twenty-Third Publications, Inc., 1977); Loretta Girzaitis, *The Church as Reflecting Community* (Mystic, Conn.: Twenty-Third Publications, Inc., 1977).

[7] Paulo Freire, *Pedagogy of the Oppressed*, trans. Myra B. Ramas (New York: Continuum Publishing Corp., 1970).

Chapter 8

[1] Joint Educational Development has recently published Phyllis C. White, *The Broadly Graded Group: A Manual for Children in the Church* (Memphis, Tenn.: Board of Christian Education, Cumberland Presbyterian Church, 1981). The unit plan under which the Lutheran Church in America materials are published would permit a religious education group that had ten children in grades one to six to choose three units of study (for grades one to two, three to four, five to six) on the same theme, such as the church, the life of Jesus, or living in families. These materials would then become resources from which teachers could choose materials to fit the needs of children who were at different learning levels.

[2] Silver Burdett Co. materials use striking illustrations from classical art, both on the covers and in the contents of its high school courses. The Lutheran Church in America has a sixth grade course on Jesus in poetry and art and one on the Advent/Christmas experience that also centers in art.

Chapter 9

[1] This and related matters are questioned in my article, "Will Ecumenical Curriculum Work?" *The Christian Century*, April 26, 1978.

Index